Dr. Patricia Carrin
researcher and highly
in the field of Energy

M000308711

Formally a lecturer in the Department of Psychology at Princeton University, she is presently an Associate Clinical Professor of Psychiatry at the University of Medicine and Dentistry-Robert Wood Johnson Medical School in New Jersey, where she instructs medical students on how to relate to patients in a manner that honors the patient's dignity as a human being.

Her widely acclaimed, medically approved, modern meditation method, Clinically Standardized Meditation (CSM) is used by organizations throughout the world, and she is a pioneer in the field of EFT (Emotional Freedom Techniques), and is one of a handful of EFT practitioners worldwide to be designated an EFT Founding Master by Gary Craig, Founder of EFT. In this area, she is the originator of the well-known EFT Choices Method which represents a major advance in this field and in recent years her work has extended to include the spiritual dimension of human beings and animals as well.

At present she divides her professional time between work with clients, teaching, writing, and the challenge of creating innovative teaching materials that extend our present reach and bring inspiration to many people.

Also by Dr. Patricia Carrington

The Book of Joy, 2016 – present, Kendall Park, NJ, Pace Educational Systems

A Guide to Tappy Bear, 2008 - 2012, Kendall Park, NJ, Pace Educational System

Discover the Power of Meridian Tapping, 2008, The Tapping Solution, New York, The Tapping Solution

Multiply the Power of EFT: 52 New Ways to Use EFT That Most People Don't Know About. 2007 - present, Kendall Park, NJ, Pace Educational Systems

The EFT Choices Manual, 2000 - present, Pace Educational Systems

Releasing, 1984 – present, New York, William Morrow & Co, and Kendall Park, NJ, Pace Educational Systems

The Book of Meditation (also published as Freedom in Meditation), 1976 – present, Kendall Park, NJ, Pace Educational Systems

THE SECRET INNER LIFE OF PETS

A Leading Psychologist and an Animal Communicator

bring you the love and wisdom of animals

by

Dr. Patricia Carrington, Ph.D.

with Karen Anderson

This Book is dedicated to
Dandy Carrington...
and to all those who have ever
had their own "Dandy"

"Dandy"
August 1999 - May 2015

My Thanks...

I want to thank my Developmental Editor, Lynn M. Johnson, for her dedicated work in helping me to assemble and summarize Karen Anderson's information as it was transmitted to me in a series of telephone interviews and as derived from Karen's book, *Hear All Creatures*. She most ably helped me construct many technical aspects of the interior of this book throughout the preparation of this book.

Lynn's love of pets of diverse and sometimes unusual kinds (she presently enjoys the companionship of Easter-Egger chickens at her home in addition to her Chihuahua dog, Precious) has been apparent throughout the preparation of this book.

Thank you, Lynn!

Table of Contents

PART ONE

THE SECRET
INNER LIFE OF PETS

PART TWO

HELPFUL CHOICES
FOR PET OWNERS

PART THREE

THE RESOURCES SECTION

PART ONE

THE SECRET INNER LIFE OF PETS

CHAPTER ONE

Lessons From A Seeing-Eye Cat

The kitten "Ginger" was born in an abandoned orange crate in the storage room of the only grocery store in town. Her mother was "professionally employed" there to catch mice.

The minute my grandmother walked into the back room to test the freshness of the apples, she spotted the calico kitten with the beautiful white ruff around her neck. This baby cat became ours when "Ma," said to Tony the grocer, "We'd be glad to take that kitty off your hands."

Tony seemed relieved to have one less cat to feed and off we drove with the kitten in my arms as my grandma steered her somewhat rickety station wagon back to our home.

Ginger, the name we immediately gave to this cat because of the orange stripes that she sported, was unusually attractive. She had delicate white paws that looked as though she was wearing tiny white gloves pulled tightly over them. The most startling thing about her though were her eyes. Emerald green, they sparkled like little gems and the effect was almost hypnotic.

Pat at three years old serving "afternoon tea" to Jack, the dog who near the end of his life was guided by the seeing eye cat, Ginger

The first six months of Ginger's life were uneventful except I suppose for her almost fanatic attachment to our elderly black half-poodle-half-something-else dog, Jack, whose tangled hair covered half of his face so that he could barely see the terrain in front of him. I think Jack thought the kitten was a puppy, or at least his own child in some way, and this suited the baby cat perfectly. They were an inseparable pair.

But when she was six months old, an unfortunate event occurred.

It was close to midnight when my grandmother rushed into my bedroom brandishing a flashlight. She called out to me to accompany her as she ran outdoors because there was "a terrible catfight" right outside the house and she was afraid Ginger might be caught in it.

I was terrified at what I sensed to be a mortal danger to my kitten but I immediately got up and accompanied my grandma out of the house, still in my pajamas, what else could I do?

My grandma's fear turned out to be correct. When we got to the site of the battle, I saw a huge tomcat seemingly tearing Ginger to pieces with giant claws. She was screaming in pain as we approached, it was nightmarish.

Amazingly though "Ma" began to drive off the marauder by brandishing a broom she had grabbed on her way out of the house. When she lunged toward the cat waving it wildly and yelling at him he retreated – he did a great deal of hissing, but somehow he backed off. Then he ran into the night.

At that point, Ma turned her attention to Ginger who was obviously in much pain. Blood was gushing from one of her eyes and she was whimpering pitifully.

Ma scooped her up and brought her into the house and phoned the veterinarian, who in those days (I guess maybe it's true in some regions of the world even today) was on call 24 hours a day. When he answered the phone, he told us to get into our car immediately and drive to his home, some seven miles away. He said he would see if he could "save the kitten".

I remember holding Ginger as gently as I could manage to as we drove there. I kept talking to her, saying things like, "It's okay Ginger....I love you...it's okay..."

When Dr. Bennett came out of the house, he picked up Ginger, took one look at her, and said "I think the eye is gone but I'm going to try my best to save the cat" and he carried her into an emergency operating room he had in his garage. Ma went with him but I was told to stay in the car.

I really didn't mind because I didn't want to witness the operation. I dreaded seeing what would happen to Ginger. The result was that I willingly stayed in the car even though I was alone and frightened.

However, after a long time which seemed interminable, my curiosity was so strong that I had to find out what was happening. I got out of the car and tiptoed to the garage to peek through the window and when I did, I saw the surgeon holding Ginger on the operating table and I saw her eye that, to my horror, was hanging loosely out of its socket. I began to tremble as I watched and thought I might throw up. Fortunately, I had some strange faith in Dr. Bennett because my family had great faith in him I guess, that's the way those things work. So I left the window and found my way back to the car, and waited.

As it turned out, the vet saved Ginger and when he carried her out to the car he had, he explained to me, been able to place her eye back into its socket and hold it in place with a tight bandage that remained in place for many days. Although Ginger was never again able to see out of that eye she at least had two eyes for humans to look at – even though one of them was cockeyed.

For a week or two after the surgery Ginger seemed to be almost totally blind and was bumping into the furniture right and left. But animals tend to recover much faster than humans from surgery and as her health returned she became a beautiful cat again –with one cockeyed eye, but still beautiful...

I'm telling you about this incident because I believe that Ginger's temporary blindness at that time may have been the reason for the extraordinary thing that we witnessed later on.

Within the next few months, our dog Jack, elderly to begin with, began to lose his eyesight. His handicap soon increased markedly, so that when he was inside the house, he was colliding with the furniture almost constantly.

I was very worried about Jack. At that time, we happened to be renting a summer house on a highway busy with speeding cars, and Jack was used to having the run of the property because he had good common sense and was always careful to avoid the road. With his increasing loss of sight, however, we obviously could no longer let him out by himself, fearing he no longer would know where the road was.

Until an unexpected thing happened...

Jack, it seems, was given a "seeing-eye dog" in the form of a cat to take care of him.

To our family's amazement and that of our neighbors, little Ginger seemed keenly to sense Jack's infirmity. I thought at the time and still do, that this was because she had experienced that temporary blindness herself when she lost her eye, but perhaps it was for some other reason.

Now, wherever Jack would go, we saw that Ginger would accompany him, walking shoulder to shoulder with the wooly black dog who was three times her size. She watched him like a hawk and immediately alerted him whenever he would head toward the road.

When she saw him turn to approach the road, Ginger would instantly move in front of Jack to block his passage. By throwing her body weight in front of him, she would force him to move in an entirely different direction. She was "herding" him the way one sees shepherd dogs herding sheep, going shoulder to shoulder with him and pressing her body against him in such a way that he had to change his path and avoid the road.

Ginger was an unerring "Seeing-Eye Cat" for Jack. Time and again we saw him head towards the road only to be herded back by her. Her behavior became news throughout the community because it was obvious she afforded consistent protection to him, and Jack could live out the last days of his life free to travel the outdoors because his little guide was always with him.

Watching this at the age of 10, I realized the depth to which an animal can identify with another living being and how powerful their love and protection can be.

I also learned something important about unlimited devotion.

Before Jack finally died of a heart attack, he was in great pain, lying on the floor and screeching and Dr. Bennett rushed to our home to give him chloroform to release him from his misery. When the vet arrived, Ginger was already at Jack's side, pressing herself against him as he lay yelping on the floor and kicking his feet futilely. We actually had to drag her off of him to allow the doctor to examine him.

She was fiercely protective and a little while later we had to hold her back from trying to force her way into the garage where the doctor was helping Jack out of his suffering through euthanasia. Jack at that point gave in and the subsequent loss of him drove Ginger frantic and for days following his departure, she stayed outside right by that garage, still a guardian of her beloved companion.

Through that experience, I was introduced to one of the most magnificent characteristics of the animal kingdom – their devotion to the object of their love, a quality chronicled in classic stories of animals who actually gave their lives to save those to whom they had extended their love and protection. You are all familiar with those stories. They are not myths but reality.

What is so important is that the loving beings that are our pets often bring forth in us as well some remarkable qualities that our human society may not encourage very much. I have seen outwardly very tough people crumble when their pets are in danger, stalwart people weep unabashedly when a beloved dog or other animal dies, children go into mourning when they are parted from their pet and have repeatedly observed these things affecting people's entire lives. So often our pets bring out in us our own capacity to love without reservation and this is one of the main reasons, I think, that we treasure them.

In the next chapter, we will consider an important question that may well occur to you as you read this book. How does it happen that a psychologist (myself in this case) who has been engaged in rigorous scientific research for many years, has become interested in investigating such a relatively unusual subject as animal communication?

This leads us directly to the story of my cat Dandy who, at the age of 16 years, passed away in the spring of 2015, and with his passing gave me the gift of this book.

CHAPTER TWO

How A Departed Pet Inspired This Book

In the summer of 2015, my cat that I loved dearly, Dandy, was failing. When he had completed the examinations and the tests, the vet told me that Dandy had intractable colon cancer and that I was to take him home, give him love, and see to it that he had the best possible quality of life during his remaining time with me. He said that I would know when it was no longer worth the pain and struggle for him and that when I felt that his life was no longer worthwhile, to bring Dandy in to be euthanized.

Because of my closeness to my cat, this idea seemed almost impossible and I knew that we would be going through a new phase of our relationship as I tried to help him handle the increasing awkwardness of his illness. He was a very dignified cat, as many cats are, and I could see that he wanted to keep his disability to himself as much as possible.

So I took him home and we coped with this difficult challenge as best we could. However, about a month later there came a point when Dandy was in such obvious pain that I finally asked him - I had a habit of speaking to him in sentences even though I was not sure that he could understand my words - "Do you want to continue on here with me now? Or do you want to be relieved of all this and just move on to a much more comfortable place?"

Since he couldn't answer in human language, I then instructed him this way, "Dandy, if you'd like to go now, I can help you by taking you to the vet who will be able to help you leave. If you want me to take you to the vet you will have to give me a signal. If you want me to take you to the vet for this then I am asking you to walk from here (we were in the living room) to the foyer and go to the front door and wait there for me. But – if you would rather stay with me for a while longer then I want you to walk up the long hallway instead, go into my office, and sit down there and wait for me."

That's all I said and for a few minutes after I had spoken Dandy did absolutely nothing. Then he slowly got up and walked gradually, one step at a time, into the foyer and seated himself at about an 8-foot distance from the front door, simply looking at the door with a quiet gaze.

I came into the foyer to watch him and waited there.

For several minutes Dandy remained absolutely still, then very gradually he got up and, slowly, approached the front door. When he reached the door he seated himself in front of it and remained there, very still, for perhaps five minutes. Then he got up again, turned, and walked slowly up the long hallway to the kitchen, passing my little office without pausing, and only glancing briefly at it. He did not enter the office.

It seemed to me that he was giving me the message that he wanted to be helped to pass away but since it was not clear that this was the case, I called the vet and made an appointment for the euthanasia but made it for several days in the future - for Friday. This gave me three days to make the final decision; I could always cancel the appointment. What troubled me greatly was that I kept asking myself, "How do I know if it wasn't just my imagination that Dandy was giving me this signal?" His life depended upon how I interpreted this.

What happened next drove me to find an animal communicator to help me decide.

The following day, as I was working at my computer, Dandy entered my office and came over to where I was sitting. He reared up on his hind legs, placed his front paws on my knees, and dug his claws firmly into my blue jeans. He did this in such a way that he did not scratch me or hurt me at all, and yet he anchored himself so powerfully to me that I could scarcely move.

He gazed intently straight into my eyes and did not avert his gaze for even a second. It was clear that he was asking something of me.

I told him I knew he wanted me to do something and I was trying to understand, and that I loved him greatly. That is all I could think to do.

Actually, during these last few days on more than one occasion he came over to me and held me still with his claws (without hurting me), and each time he looked deep and long into my eyes with that intense gaze.

His plea was so obvious that at that point I decided to consult a professional animal communicator to help me with my decision. I had never done this before, not because I do not believe in their effectiveness but because I had never actually had a reason to do so.

So I tried to reach several animal communicators who were highly recommended by friends, but it was a person I found after an independent search on the Internet who, as soon as I first heard her speak on her voicemail, I knew to be the person I would consult.

I made an appointment with this communicator, Karen Anderson, to discuss the possible euthanasia. Friday was only two days off at this point and so Karen requested that I immediately email her a photo of Dandy, but told me not to tell her anything about him or what my questions were. I was just to send the picture by itself so that she could look at it in an unbiased manner.

When a day later I connected with Karen by phone, the first thing she said to me was, "Please don't tell me anything about Dandy. I want to connect with him directly first."

I asked whether he needed to be in the room with me when she did this, which he wasn't, and she said it wasn't necessary and that she was already sensing him. Karen does her work by remote-sensing and almost always works by telephone. She was actually far from us geographically. I live on the East coast of the United States, and she was in Washington state which is on the West Coast, 3,000 miles away.

After a relatively short pause, Karen said, "Dandy is telling me that he feels as though he had been hit in the stomach with a baseball bat! He is begging you to take him away from this pain." I had not told her yet that he had abdominal cancer and that his stomach area was so bloated that it was truly distorted and he could barely manage to sit down, but that clearly fit with her description of his being hit with a baseball bat in the stomach. I was shocked.

I then told her how he had been coming into the room lately, digging his claws firmly into my blue jeans, and staring up at me with that intent pleading gaze. Had he been saying the same thing to me that as he was now conveying to Karen? "Get me out of this Pat! Get me out of this!"

Yes, she said, he had.

I then told Karen his whole medical history and went on to discuss the question of euthanasia with her. She helped me understand how animals experience that, which was comforting to me - I will tell you about that later - and said that Dandy said to tell me that I had been wonderful to him during his illness and there was nothing more that I could have done and he thanked me with all his heart for all I had been doing. He also told her to tell me that he and I would never be separated, even after he passed.

A little later in the call, however, Karen suddenly told me that Dandy had just broken into the conversation to ask her to "tell Pat that after I pass away I want to help her with her work."

I was startled by this statement and somewhat confused. While I had gone along with the conversation I was having with Karen thus far, being as open-minded as I could in response to what she was saying and clearly impressed with her accurate assessment of Dandy's physical condition (the extreme pain in his abdomen which corresponded exactly to the location of his colon cancer - and which I had told her nothing about) this idea of the book seemed so far out as to be almost ridiculous.

Dandy was a wonderful cat to be sure, but he was an animal. How could he possibly help me with my work, which involves practicing psychology, creating recorded materials, writing books, and working with human patients? This seemed totally far-fetched. However, I was impressed with Karen's integrity and knew that at this point she had no idea what profession I was in or how a cat could possibly help with me with it.

The day after my conversation with Karen, I was talking to a good friend who is very sensitive and for years has been telling me about her close contact with a spirit guide whom she calls "Dear One." The latter has always seemed to give my friend unusually accurate assessments of current situations, and this time my friend told me that her guide was telling her that "Dandy wants to help Pat write a book."

Now I was even more puzzled. A book contributed to by Dandy didn't make any sense to me, and as you read about this you may want to honor this concept as just a possibility and decide later whether you wish to believe that it represents a reality. Actually, when reading this book, you need not believe anything that does not feel authentic to you in order to benefit surprisingly from the information it will bring to you concerning the inner life of pets. I suggest you just "coast along" as you read the book and as much as possible remain open to pretty much anything without judgment at this point.

To continue with this incident, a few hours after talking with my friend, an idea for a new book popped into my mind unexpectedly, it was to be a book about the love and wisdom of animals and how they can teach us incredible lessons.

This was certainly an unexpected turn of events. I had never dreamed I would be writing a book about animals. The books I had published in the past were on meditation and other important stress management methods for people.

However, I have always been fascinated by the ability of animals to sense what is going on with us and how they often help us in so many intangible ways. As Dandy and I went through his last days together, the idea of writing this book was beginning to become a reality for me, despite the "always rational" nature of my life-long work and the topics of my previous books.

I did take Dandy to the veterinarian for euthanasia as planned on Friday, which happened to be the day of Good Friday just before Easter, commemorating the crucifixion, which I had not realized before I made the appointment.

I remained with Dandy – the vet left us alone in the room together - as he quietly passed away, and a good friend of mine later took me with her to a service at her church after his departure, which seemed very appropriate for this occasion. I was able to feel calm and peaceful after he died because of Karen's information about how quickly the experience of the euthanasia itself passes from their memory after the animal leaves their body. This was immensely reassuring to me.

CHAPTER THREE

The Story That Led Up To Now

There is always a story behind every book, and it has often commenced many years before the writing of it.

Throughout my childhood, I was fascinated by the unpredictable ways of both people and animals. This is probably why I became a psychologist absorbed in an effort to understand the puzzle that is life, even though I have been trained for a profession where I work to be helpful only to my own species – human beings.

In addition to being a psychologist working with people, I was also trained as a researcher where I had to painstakingly engage in rational thinking at all times. I was involved in studying and observing human beings while I was simultaneously attempting to help them. This combination does not always work well however and can cause some inner conflicts.

Actually, a conflict would sometimes arise between my rational, scientific self and my intuitive self, which was responding to a seemingly unseen aspect of life, a part of me that was actually half buried for many years as I worked as a traditional psychologist. However, it did creep in periodically and in recent years, it has proved to be of major importance.

For example, in the 1970's I developed an absorbing interest in meditation about which I wrote a very well received book, Freedom in Meditation, and subsequently other books that dealt with the so-called "energy psychology" techniques that move us forward in our understanding of the mystery of life.

My intuitive sense of "something else" other than the obvious objectively known things in life was, in fact, the reason I decided to enroll in an unusual online workshop offered in the spring of 2014 that promised to teach me how to meet my "spirit guides"– of all things for a "logical scientific person" to contemplate!

I remember telling myself at that time that the guides would in a sense represent my own inner wisdom, and in fact, that proved to be correct.

A gifted spiritual leader, Gil Alan, taught this workshop, and its training so profoundly changed my life that I became open to a whole new realm of understanding after immersing myself in its wisdom for just the eight weeks of the course. It inspired a conversation with my soul that opened a new era for me that has profoundly influenced both my personal and work life (*if you would like to know more about this life-changing workshop see the description in the Resource Section in Part Three of the book*).

Having experienced this newfound realm of understanding while Dandy was still with me, after he died, I decided to connect with the animal communicator, Karen Anderson, who had so ably assisted me at the time of his passing and ask her if she would like to work with me on a book that I felt compelled to write, one that seemed to have been suggested by my cat, Dandy!

Karen agreed to share with me some of her amazing stories and insights to go into such a book and so our work together began.

And now I invite you to experience a similar realm of understanding, on whatever level is comfortable for you, as you read about the unusual conversations that Karen Anderson conducts with animals, both living and those who have passed away. Her incredible way of communicating with animals can teach you many things about your own pets and the amazing lessons they may hold for you. It may help you experience insights that even in your closest moments with your beloved animal you may not have yet suspected.

As you read her stories in this book, you will personally decide whether you want to view the experiences Karen describes as the truth (i.e. the way things are), or prefer to view them as only reasonable possibilities, or whether you want to see them as ingenious inventions of the human mind which nevertheless can help you deepen your own understanding of your pet.

Whichever way you choose to view these accounts will work for you. Even if you were to look at this book as only a fascinating storybook it would bring you closer, probably a great deal closer, to the animals in your life.

I say this because I think there is an intuitive understanding within every one of us who has ever loved an animal that tells us that our "pet" is not a mere possession of ours, but a soul seeking beauty and joy and love even as we do. I suspect you would not have chosen to read this particular book if you did not sense that truth.

... And now, we will go on to the next stage in our exploration of animal communication as you learn about Karen Anderson and how this gifted woman came to "talk" with animals in the first place!

CHAPTER FOUR

Karen's Personal Journey

You may be wondering how skilled animal communicator, Karen Anderson, learned to hold conversations with animals that are just like the conversations humans have with each other, in the first place.

Here is her story.

Karen grew up in a small town in Southern California and, as far as she knows, her ability to talk with animals began as soon as she began to understand language, and perhaps even before that.

One of the reasons (but by no means the only one) for her ease in talking to animals may have been the influence of the Walt Disney studios on her life.

Karen's family lived only a 30-minute ride from Disneyland in California and this enchanted land played a major role in her formative years.

Her very favorite exhibit there, she remembers, was called the "Tiki Room". In it, birds, flowers, and animals sang and talked to the children who visited its magical living world. This exhibit beckoned to her and she fought to return to it as often as possible.

In addition to her experiences at Disneyland, Karen also immersed herself in, and in a sense "lived" through the Disney animated films most of which, she points out, depicted animals talking throughout.

It, therefore, seemed quite natural to her that the same thing was happening with the many animals in her own home. Her playful affectionate interaction with them was the center of her life.

Enter Prince

Karen (in forefront reaching out to touch him) laying claim to her beloved Prince as the family poses.

Karen was especially enchanted by her friendship with her dog Prince, a black and white collie with a luxurious coat and magnificent ruff who, from the first, was her constant companion. Prince would talk with her and she with him many times each day, and he was endlessly patient, often agreeing good naturedly to allow her to pretend he was a horse, put a blanket on his back, and lead him around a pretend "coral".

This was in the days before she attended school. When she entered first grade, the school didn't want their pupils bringing dogs into the classroom so she soon learned not to do so. And this reminds me of the Mother Goose nursery rhyme:

Mary had a Little Lamb
Its fleece was white as snow.
And everywhere that Mary went,
the Lamb was sure to go...

Such child-animal companionships can be all consuming and seem like the only order of things.

Not surprisingly, for the first few years of her life, Karen assumed that all other children and adults had exactly the same ability to talk with animals as she did.

She was soon to find out that this was not the case however through an incident that occurred when her dog Prince became ill.

Prince slept in her room at night but one night he was keeping her awake with constant heavy panting. Prince was clearly not himself so she asked him what was wrong.

"I want to sleep on the cool floor." He answered.

She realized Prince was referring to the floor in the hall and she knew something was quite wrong for him to want to do that.

"Take me to sleep on the cool tile floor," Prince said to her, "and you come with me."

Karen obediently opened her bedroom door, went with Prince into the hall, and lay down beside him as he stretched out on the floor, groaning in pain. She rested her head on his belly and could hear an immense rumbling going on within it. In answer to her question about this, he told her he had a "BIG Pain in my tummy".

In the morning, her parents found Karen curled up asleep on the hall floor with Prince, and were shocked. "What's the matter with you sleeping on the floor like that with Prince?" her mother asked her.

"Prince is sick," she answered. "He says his tummy hurts a lot. I think he needs the dog doctor.

Her mother dismissed this idea by saying, "I think you're pretending that he said that to you, dogs don't talk."

Karen didn't understand what her mother was talking about and insisted.

"Mommy, he says it hurts a lot."

Her mother shooed her off, but Prince did not get better as the week went on. As it turned out her parents eventually did have to take him to the veterinarian who diagnosed Prince as suffering from a pancreatitis that was severe and painful. He was treated for it and eventually, with the medicine, he recovered.

The family didn't give Karen any credit for knowing about Prince's illness, however, but chose to ignore the whole incident.

After that, she was careful not to tell her parents about her conversations with animals. However, she still assumed, incorrectly of course, that all children talked with animals the way she did - until she found out that this too was not so.

She came face-to-face with this bewildering fact when she was eight years old. At that time, she was best friends with a little girl named Lori who had a horse that she kept in the local stables and Karen was crazy about horses. One day when they were riding Lori's pony together, bareback, the pony kept bucking and they didn't know why. When Karen asked the horse the reason he was bucking, he answered her by saying that his back hurt today and it hurt him too much to have the two of them on him.

When Karen relayed this message to Lori, the latter scoffed at it.

"Đon't be silly!" She said. "Only a horse can talk to another horse!"

"Doesn't your horse tell you when something's wrong with him?" Karen asked, amazed.

Lori simply dismissed this idea, "Of course not!" she said.

After that, Karen decided to conceal her talks with animals from her friends as well as her family. Although to Karen, this seemed to be the way people and animals helped each other, and it made perfect sense to her, she now realized that other people didn't feel the same way she did and so she couldn't talk with animals in front of them.

But the fun she had connecting with animals continued in full force, in secret, until one fateful day when Karen was in third grade.

She was sitting on her front porch when she spotted an adorable kitten on the other side of the road that was clearly a stray – Karen knew all the other animals in the neighborhood. So she called out to the cat telepathically, "Come over and play with me Kitty!" and the cute orange and white cat clearly heard her but was at first afraid to venture out into the street.

Because she wanted so much to play with this fun new companion, however, Karen called to the kitten repeatedly in her mind to come over and play - she often talked silently in her mind to animals, as well as out loud.

The kitten continued to stare at Karen with large round wondering eyes but still would not venture onto the road. Karen called her again telepathically the way she often conversed with animals and she knew that the kitten understood what she said.

Finally, the kitten lost her fears and decided to heed Karen's pleas and come over and play and she tentatively stepped out on the road and then scampered forward with increasing confidence.

To Karen's shock, however, the kitten never arrived at her side of the road because at exactly that moment a large brown car swerved around the corner, seemingly out of nowhere, and in an instant had struck the kitten full force and tossed it up into the air to fall writhing in pain on the street right in front of Karen's eyes. She witnessed this whole incident.

She could do nothing to save the kitten from its pain and the baby animal soon died. Karen felt almost as though the car had hit her. She was acutely aware that she was helpless to do anything for the cat and now prefers not to remember that moment in any detail to this day, because it caused her such overwhelming distress and deep guilt. She thought that she had killed the kitten by insisting it come over and play with her. Everything that happened was, in her mind, her fault. She had done it!

Karen then promised herself, right at that moment when she was eight years old, that she would never again talk with animals. She never wanted to hurt another animal that way again, so she swore to herself she would not use her apparently unusual gift of talking to them.

From then on, she did her best to keep this vow, purposely stifling the wonderful loving conversations she had had with animals, for the next two decades. Then finally, many years later when she had become a deputy sheriff in Park County, Colorado, she discovered a new use for her unusual ability to communicate with animals and allowed herself to use that precious ability again.

Karen's Career as a Police Officer

Karen's career in law enforcement was not an easy one but she learned much from it.

Initially, she was sworn in as a Reserve Deputy and volunteered for the Animal Control unit which was administered by the Sheriff's office. The sergeant had seen how committed she was when she was riding along with the animal control officers and how well she did with these calls. At that point, he suggested that she consider becoming a deputy and said, "you'll make a good cop!"

Soon after, Karen started riding along with the deputies and from there caught the law enforcement "bug" and went to the Police Academy where she graduated with the Top Award in "Arrest Control".

As soon as she was appointed, she found herself the target of unrelenting "testing" from an all-male group of police officers. However, it was through her experience on the police force that she found, to her own surprise, that she was now able to talk with animals again – these were animals at the scenes of domestic crimes. These animals could easily identify the real culprit for her each time and this made her an extraordinarily effective rookie for investigating criminal activity.

Karen explains her success with the domestic violence cases by saying that "animals don't lie, they are honest, forthcoming, and don't have human agendas, so they would tell me what I needed to know for my police report and it inevitably turned out to be a correct lead."

While she carefully did not tell the other officers how she was obtaining the information she managed to collect when conducting her investigations, they soon realized that she had some uncanny ability to know things about cases that they did not know, and they used it to good advantage.

Karen remembers one harrowing incident, during her time on the police force, in which communication from animals played an essential role.

She had been undergoing intense "testing" by the department who had, on a dark autumn night, sent out four patrol cars to apprehend an armed suspect who had fled the scene after he rolled his vehicle off the side of a rural country road. They believed he was hiding in the wooded area somewhere and three other deputies sped off in one direction and told Karen to go in the opposite direction - alone – in her own patrol car. She was to be without any protection from a backup car.

On foot and alone in the darkness, Karen took up a shielded position behind some trees, when, in the large field in front of her she saw four deer slowly making their way toward her in the moonlight. As she sat quietly, the deer lifted their heads and then turned their heads in one direction, all of them pointing their noses toward a grassy field to her right. It was in exactly the opposite direction from where the rest of the deputies were searching for the suspect.

The night was perfectly still and not a sound could be heard. Karen noticed the deer approaching closer and closer from her left, and when they got within a few feet of her, on a whim she asked one of them telepathically "Where is he? Can you see him?"

The answer came immediately, "Behind that log." the deer said, which was about 25 yards away to her right.

On hearing that, Karen cautiously approached, staying hidden along the tree line with her weapon aimed toward the log.

"Sheriff's Office! Show me your hands!" she cried out. At first, there was no response but suddenly, to her own surprise. Karen watched as two human hands popped up from the tall grass right behind the log.

"Don't shoot!" came the man's voice as he slowly rose from his hiding spot.

She then radioed the rest of the officers and directed them to her location. "I've got him at gunpoint," she said.

Within minutes the officers arrived with a shocked look on their faces. The suspect was taken into custody without incident. Her fellow officers had no idea Karen had been directed to the spot by the deer but all were amazed that she had found the suspect in such a vast wooded area.

After that, Karen continued to sharpen her intuitive abilities during her law enforcement career. She did this by gathering information from the animals that were on the scenes of crimes. Eventually, however, she realized that working with animals was her real calling, and thus began another phase of her life

Noah the Dove

Karen was eagerly seeking all the information she could gather on animal communication and trying to practice it as often as she could, but since she was just starting out she had to rely on family and friends for the loan of their pets to work with in her practice sessions. However, when she did this she sensed, to her surprise and disappointment, that many of these people were less than excited about her habit of talking with animals. In fact, one of her closest friends at that time became suddenly distant and began making disparaging remarks about what she was doing.

The negative comments of people who were important to her upset Karen so much that she gradually found herself practicing her animal communication skills less and less. She became increasingly quiet at that time and did not share her fledgling work involving animals with any but a few select people.

Her reticence about her work was about to change, however, due to her meeting with the dove.

Karen was sitting on a deck at a Fourth of July barbecue when the host of the party, who happened to know about her unusual practice of talking to animals, asked her if she would be willing to visit with a neighbor's bird that had been rescued from the mouth of one of his neighbor's cats and they were nursing it back to health.

Karen's instinct to help was immediately kindled and she willingly went to the house next door to see what she could do for the bird. Terry, the neighbor involved, greeted her with relief and in a few moments returned to the room where Karen waited, with a beautiful white dove perched on her index finger.

Karen extended her own finger to this quiet dignified dove and to her surprise he stepped onto it without hesitation. The bird continued to sit there perfectly still, even though excited children were running through the room begging to pet him.

The children wanted to know whether the bird liked his food, if his cage was right, and they had other burning questions. But at the request of their mother, the whole family now gathered near Karen to find out what this little dove "has to say".

Karen began by silently saying a special prayer addressed to all animals, which contained a blessing for them and asked the dove's permission to communicate. Before she had the opportunity to ask him any questions, however, he said to her, "I've been expecting you."

"You've been expecting me?" she asked him quietly in her mind, surprised at this declaration.

"Indeed..." he said "...the human who talks to animals... I've been expecting you. Tell them the food is fine, but please keep the cats away from the cage. I would also like it to be higher up."

Karen told the family what the dove had said about his food and Terry confirmed that the dove was being housed in a dog crate on the floor and that the cats could get their paws inside of it.

Since Karen wasn't quite sure what the dove meant by "I've been expecting you" though, she did not mention that to the family.

"He doesn't want the cats near him." she said, "perhaps you can raise his cage a bit?".

One of the children then broke in excitedly "Where did he come from? Find out where he came from."

To Karen's surprise, the dove answered quietly, "From up above."

More questions then came tumbling out of the children "Did he come from a family? Does he want to go home?"

"I come from heaven above." The dove continued. Then he said, obviously addressing only Karen, "I am here to meet with you. I've been waiting for this moment." He then remained quiet, still on the end of her index finger.

At that moment, Karen had an intense experience which she describes as almost overwhelming. She felt a rush of energy fill her body at the same time as the family's voices drifted into oblivion so that she literally could hear them no more – she could then only hear what the dove said.

He looked directly at her with those keen eyes of a little bird, and declared, "I am here to tell you to follow your heart. You are to follow your path with animals. It is your calling." Then he added, "You know in your heart that this is the right thing to do."

As he talked, questions were still pouring in from the children who crowded around them but Karen couldn't take her eyes off the dove.

"You are up against adversity and negativity, isn't that true?" The dove asked, and Karen immediately recalled the disparaging comments she had been experiencing from those whom she had told about her new career.

Tears now came to Karen's eyes. They were tears of relief that somebody understood.

"You have been getting away from doing this lately, haven't you?" the dove continued.

At that point, the recent uncomfortable events of her life came into her mind as though she were watching a movie and she saw herself from an unusual perspective, "almost as though I was watching the past happen again." And when she experienced this she felt her fears resurface and could feel the pain she was experiencing "in the movie" as she watched her friends make disparaging comments about her relationship with animals.

The little white dove then said, "My child........". then he hesitated and asked gently, "Have you ever been touched by the hand of God?"

As he spoke these words, Karen could feel a great warmth emanating from his feet and radiating into her hand upon which he still perched. It spread up her arm and then to her shoulder. This warmth was extraordinarily peaceful and comforting.

"Well, I don't think so. I think I would remember that" she said, uncertain as to just how to answer.

"Consider yourself touched by His hand now." said the dove.

Karen stood riveted to the spot as the dove spoke to her, even though she knew the children were clamoring for more answers. She did not know how to tell them that his messages were actually meant for her, not them.

"Ask him what he wants his name to be" one of the children was demanding.

"Tell them I would like a name with dignity," the Dove answered.

Karen repeated his words, "He would like a name with dignity" she said softly and then the dove began fluttering his wings as though getting ready to fly away, which signaled to her that the meeting was ended.

Karen stood transfixed and then slowly walked out of the house after thanking the family and making sure they would keep in contact.

The outcome of this visit is now history for Karen, and from that time on she embraced her animal communication career with a courage born of certainty.

The dove remained with the adoptive family and Karen discovered later that the family had named the bird "Noah" and he has lived with them to this day, in a lovely cage, high above the cats.

This incident brought Karen back onto her path. She now embraced animal communication openly as her career and was excited to talk about it to anyone.

Questions This Raises

These events led up to Karen's present work with animals and their owners, and her story obviously leaves us with some questions. One of them is – are we perhaps all animal communicators at heart, but simply don't know that we are?

Theoretically, this is, of course, possible but it's hard to determine. We do know that in certain societies, an open communication between animals and humans is actually the norm, not the exception, however. This is said to be true, for example, of the aborigines of Australia who have been known for their telepathic ability to talk with animals and they admit such ability freely and naturally.

It is also reported to have been a highly developed trait in many Native American tribes who had great respect for animals, wearing their hides and their feathers to adopt their strength and wisdom. Other primitive peoples have also been described as having this same ability.

A disbelief in this kind of gift in our present Western civilization is what Karen had poignantly discovered early in her life and again when she first decided to work with animals as her career. It was this disbelief in what she knew to be true that had delayed the realization of her true calling for many years.

Another question we might ask is whether this kind of communication may only be possible with human beings and domestic animals who are so familiar with the ways of humans that in a sense they have been trained to respond in a human-like way.

This does not seem to be the case, however. When Karen was a little child and open to a connection with animals without any self-consciousness or reservations, her conversations were not limited to domestic animals at all. Aside from cats, dogs, parrots and her much-loved horses, which were species whose lives are closely interwoven with human beings, Karen was fascinated by talking with lizards, snakes, and other reptiles, as well as with birds, fish, and insects. All of them, she reports, were eager to talk with her and had wonderful information to impart.

Interestingly, she points out that in many ancient and primitive societies there may not have been an established hierarchy of lower animals vs. higher animals as is taken for granted in our present society, with the human race viewed as being at the pinnacle of the animal kingdom as we picture it to be. While we need not really be concerned with that question here, it is perhaps something to think about.

Here in this book, we will be considering those animals that are so connected with humans as to be almost indistinguishable from them at times – the ones we usually adopt as our pets.

What are the Childhood Experiences of Other Animal Communicators?

Their reports interest me greatly as a psychologist.

In my informal contacts with them (I have conducted no formal research in this area) a number of animal communicators have reported that they had some of their wisest most truly understanding connections with animals other than with humans in early life, and that the time they spent with them was sometimes even more meaningful than that with their own human family. Not surprisingly, they learned to respond telepathically to the communications of animals and learned how to communicate back to these animals, and often the conversations that they experienced with non-humans were more meaningful to them than any exchanges with any other living creatures.

We are, of course, closest to what we have known. Most animal communicators have experienced animals as trustworthy and consistently loving beings during their childhood world and considered animals their "family."

But despite their closeness to animals, communicators may at times have to struggle to decipher some of the messages they are being "sent". We will next look at the special ways in which animals convey their messages and some of the problems it can cause to those unfamiliar with animal communication.

CHAPTER FIVE

Puzzling Pet Messages

Karen frequently receives puzzling messages from pets, both living and deceased, and while they often seem to make no sense to her, surprisingly they may have very personal meanings to the pet owners, as you will see in the following accounts.

Sara the Pit-Bull Reveals a Daunting Secret

This interesting story involves a woman named "Lisa" (not her real name) who drove many miles on a very hot day to consult with Karen about her pit-bull named Sara because the dog was showing highly anxious behavior. Despite all the trouble she had taken to drive to where Karen was consulting with clients in a booth at an expo, Lisa initially showed much skepticism, making it clear that she didn't even know if she "believed in any of this."

When asked what Lisa wanted to find out from her dog, who sat obediently at her side, she replied, "I don't know." Then she added, "Well, ask her if she has any messages for me."

Karen immediately connected telepathically with the dog and the first thing Sara said was a two-word phrase, "Night trauma." So, Karen reported, "Sara is telling me something about a "night trauma." Do you know what this means?"

"No, I don't think so," Lisa replied.

Again, the dog spoke to Karen and told her to repeat the words "night trauma" to Lisa.

"She's telling me again to say 'night trauma'," Karen said. "Is there something going on at night with Sara?" She knew this had to be important because the dog kept sending her the same message.

"No. Not that I can think of." Lisa answered vaguely and changed the subject. "Doesn't Sara need to be looking at you?"

Karen reassured her that Sara was just fine doing what she was doing, watching the dog races and talking to Karen at the same time. The muscular brown and white dog was sitting with her back toward Karen watching the little dogs racing back and forth in the Wiener dog races that were going on at the fairgrounds.

"Well then, is anything going on with you at night?"

"With me? Well," Lisa spoke rather slowly. "I've had some trouble sleeping lately. Sara gets up with me at night when I can't sleep."

"Sara is worried about you because of this night trauma," Karen said. "She says you're making yourself sick and upset. Do you know what she's talking about?"

Lisa stared at Karen and her eyes began to fill with tears.

"She's also telling me to tell you to stop doubting," Karen said as the messages continued to come through the dog. Although Sara was intensely watching the wiener dog races, which were the most popular event at the Expo, she kept conveying messages to Karen.

"I'm not sure what this means," Karen said "But Sara is telling me there is a big thing that you are doubting. I'm supposed to tell you to stop doubting this big thing. Again, I don't know what that means, but she says "tell her to stop doubting – stop doubting!"

On hearing this, Lisa started to sob. Karen had no idea what was happening and so she waited.

When Lisa had regained her composure, she asked, "How did you know that?"

"How did I know what?" Karen asked. She had no idea what the big thing the dog had mentioned was.

"I have been doubting God," Lisa said. "I've been doubting the existence of God, and have been losing sleep over it. How did you know that?"

Through her tears, Lisa then continued, "There was no way you could have known that. Only my good friends know. They've sent their pastors and ministers to my house to talk to me about God, and the existence of God, but I don't believe them. I don't believe what they say. There's no way you could have known that!"

"Sara told me," Karen answered quietly. "She's worried about you. She loves you."

Lisa was trembling so much that Karen and her husband who was also in the booth, allowed her to sit there quietly until she was composed. This session had shaken them all.

As Lisa left, she said, "I guess I owe you an apology. I guess I didn't realize I was causing Sara to be so upset. I never meant for that to happen."

Actually, this kind of surprise is typical of some people when they learn about the sensitivity of their pets to their own moods and emotions. Animals don't always understand what we are upset about. They just know when we're worried and they understand enough to be concerned for us. Sara had told Karen it was "something big" that was upsetting her "mom." And, it turned out that it was a very big issue in Lisa's life.

Karen's story about the dog, Sara, highlights one of the major traits that we can probably all identify in our pets – their consistent love and deep concern for those in their human family. This kind of love has a particular quality to it. It can be a lesson for many of us because it is without judgment of any kind.

Twinkie

This is an account of a departed cat named Twinkie, a buff-colored cat with white cream on its neck and chin that made her look like a "Twinkie", an American snack cake which is golden with a creamy filling. It is the first of a number of accounts I will be relaying to you of animals who have communicated with Karen after they passed on. If this fact bothers you in any way or if you find these accounts difficult to believe, I suggest you treat them as you would a parable –a symbolic story – and not feel pressured to interpret them in any particular manner. Each account will have its own message, it will express itself in its own way. You are not required to change any belief of yours or to stretch your imagination in any manner in order to learn things that will be helpful for your pet. Just read these stories with respect. They are born from a deep intuitive sensitivity that honors the spirit of animals.

Actually, there are some hidden messages in these accounts for all of us.

As Karen prepared for Twinkie's owner to call in for her session, she began to see a persistent image in her own mind of, of all things, a tube of toothpaste. Despite the fact that she was puzzled by this image she kept seeing it, over and over again. The image of toothpaste had come to her at the same time that Twinkie's energy had started to come to her, and now she couldn't get it out of her mind. It seemed "out of left field" and without any explanation.

All became clearer, however, when her client phoned and Karen inadvertently discovered that this woman had just come from a grocery store where she had purchased a tube of toothpaste, right before the session. When she removed it from her carrying bag at Karen's request, it looked exactly like the image of toothpaste Karen had seen in her mind.

But the reason for it in the first place? – why should toothpaste have any importance? – was still unclear. The image was only explained when the departed cat told Karen telepathically that she had "been there" with her mom at the grocery store the whole time and had seen her owner buy the toothpaste.

The interesting thing about her visit to the store is that this woman went only to get one thing there – toothpaste. She didn't need anything else, she just bought toothpaste, and her cat reported this exact fact through the image she was sending Karen. It took only hearing about this image to convince this client that her cat had been lovingly observing everything she did even though Twinkie was no longer living on earth. This was quite obviously the meaning of the communication – proof that her cat was with her at all times, exactly what Lisa needed to hear.

The Message in a Tape Measure

Karen was working with one of her clients, Rachel, in a follow-up session concerning her departed cat, Brie. This cat had been very young when she had suddenly died from Feline Infectious Peritonitis (FIP), a feline viral disease. It was a great shock to her owner because from the time they diagnosed it until the time the cat died was less than three weeks.

Brie was a beautiful Siamese cat with very blue eyes and was about three years old at the time of her passing. She sported a Siamese cream color body with dark black feet and tail.

When she is preparing for client sessions, Karen routinely meditates before the session to open herself to whatever information seems to want to come through, bringing the animal's energy in while she herself is in a peaceful meditative state.

This time she was sitting quietly and tuning into Brie and beginning to feel the energy of this beautiful cat that had passed on, when all of a sudden, seemingly "out of the blue", the image of a tape measure flashed into Karen's mind. It seemed to have been sent to her by Brie. There was only this one image in her mind, no words and no story to go with it.

Karen thought, "What in the world? A tape measure! Of all the things for a cat to show me!". This was not a thought that made any sense to her. So Karen asked the cat telepathically what the image was. Why was she showing her a tape measure?

Brie didn't seem to be able to answer her - she didn't know how to describe the reason. Instead, she just sent another message, "Well then, talk to my mom about the tape measure."

As Karen conducted her session with the client, she didn't mention anything about the tape measure at first, though, because she was allowing other messages to come through. In fact, almost at the end of the session, the departed cat had to remind her by sending Karen the message, "Don't forget the tape measure,". At that point, the clear image of a tape measure then flashed again into Karen's mind and she couldn't help laughing because it was, to her, "off-the-wall", of all the unimportant things to be shown – a tape measure!

But by now Karen was becoming curious about this, and asked Rachel, "What's going on? Why

am I seeing a tape measure?"

Rachel had been softly crying because they were checking in on her kitty and she was missing her deeply, even though the experience was bittersweet because the cat had been reporting that she was doing fine where she was now.

Karen continued her inquiry. "I'm seeing a tape measure." She said. "Why would I see a tape measure?"

Rachel suddenly started giggling even though it was just moments since she had been deeply sad from missing her cat.

Karen continued to question her, "What's the deal with this? Why am I seeing a tape measure?"

Rachel then cried out, "Karen, I can't believe this is happening!"

She explained that just before their appointment, she had been on the phone with her mother who lives in another state. Her mother was in the process of downsizing and sending all of her belongings out to any of her children who wanted whatever she had to send them, whether it was towels, or linens, or clothes, or whatever. She asked Rachel if she wanted some bed sheets and linens for her bed.

Rachel told her that she had a California king-sized bed and the sheets never fit because it's an odd size. Rachel's mom then said, "Well, why don't you get out a tape measure and measure the size of your mattress so that we can make sure it's the right size?"

Rachel had then taken out a tape measure from a drawer, gone into the bedroom and started measuring the size of her mattress when she spotted a special pillow that her cat Brie used to sleep on at night. The pillow was right by her headboard. As she picked up the pillow, she had become sad and said aloud, "Oh, Brie, I just wish I knew that you were here with me! I'm missing you so. I wish you could tell me that you're here with me."

She then set the pillow aside and finished measuring the mattress to make sure it was the right size for the sheets she would be receiving.

Karen now realized why Brie had shown her that image. It was proof that she had been there with her "mom" all along! The only proof that would be really convincing to her mom.

Karen and Rachel talked for quite a while after the session about how amazing it was that she had been missing Brie so much during that moment of measuring the bed near where Brie used to sleep – and Brie had then sent the perfect image to convince her Mom that she was there with her all along.

Now we will turn to another important aspect of animal communication – the degree to which trauma plays a key role in determining many puzzling pet behaviors.

CHAPTER SIX

When Trauma Is The Culprit

It has only been in the last few years that the role trauma plays in shaping the lives of both humans and animals has been fully realized. All living things have a deep instinct to avoid what seems like annihilation. People and animals will do almost anything to circumvent this and when they have a "near miss" as it is called, where they encounter a situation that they perceive as extreme danger, but still remain alive, the living organism has strange ways of coping with this.

Recently, researchers have discovered many ways in which traumatized beings are enabled to continue living effectively despite the residual terror that can be created by great danger. One way to cope with extreme shock is to almost literally freeze in place and become immobile. In a sense, the animal or person doing this is anesthetizing themselves, and later, as they recover, they may go into a state of intense trembling or show other symptoms of extreme stress as they come out of the protective "anesthesia" that trauma initially creates.

One of the most distressing effects of trauma is a disorder known as Post-Traumatic Stress Disorder (or PTSD). It is probably as prevalent in animals as it is in people and represents a malfunction of the whole system as a result of the shock that has occurred at the time the unfortunate incident happened.

In terms of psychotherapy for humans or the kind of work that animal communicators do to help animals, severe trauma is frequently the hidden culprit when it comes to odd behaviors that the owners of an animal and sometimes even veterinarians and other trained professionals cannot readily explain.

Adya

This account concerns an unfortunate cat that experienced the continuing distress of a condition that veterinary science could not seem to help her with. It was causing great distress to her devoted owner, who finally brought her to Karen in a desperate attempt to discover the cause of Adya's obsessive and painful "over-grooming" to the point of almost mutilating herself with this bizarre behavior.

Adya was pulling her hair out of her body in large tufts with her teeth and nails and thereby creating bloody patches all over her body. Karen was actually shocked when she first saw the photograph of this cat – she looked seriously mutilated.

Her owner, Linda, had already taken her to numerous specialists in the veterinary community and a number of them were holistic veterinarians. All of them were baffled because they could not find the cause of Adya's frantic tearing out of her hair. It made the animal's life a misery and, much against her will because she much loved this cat, Linda was now fighting off the thought of euthanasia. She was forced to consider it however because Adya's life had become a nightmare.

When Linda phoned, Karen was quickly able to connect with the cat and as soon as she did she felt a sinking feeling as though she herself had been abandoned in alien territory. She later learned that the animal had been a stray for a long time, separated much too soon after birth from her mother and handed from owner to owner in a long series of adoptive homes, none of which worked for her until Adya finally landed with Linda, who immediately gave her the loving care she so needed.

Quite soon in the telepathic conversation Karen was conducting with Adya, the cat said abruptly, "Every time I love someone, they get rid of me." It seems that "being gotten rid of" was all this animal had known. Adya then added, "Whenever I open up to them and show my love, they get rid of me."

It turned out that Adya was responding to Linda's constant questioning of herself as to whether, in fact, she was the "wrong owner" for this cat. Out of her love for her, Linda was wondering whether she was the reason why the cat was tearing herself to pieces.

This very questioning on the part of Linda struck terror into the cat's heart and she began even more fiercely to try to care for herself in the only way that cats know – by grooming!. She had never had proper grooming as a kitten because she was separated too soon from the mother, causing a deep trauma. She had never had a purring mother or littermates cuddling up to her– she had had no loving protection at all.

As far as Karen could see, Adya had tried to heal all these wounds of abandonment by trying to calm her own self, and she had done this by overdoing her own self-care in the form of unceasing grooming. She was reaching out to bring to herself some sense of comfort, belonging, and mothering. At the same time, she became even more alarmed as she watched her owner, to whom she so desperately wanted to be attached, begin to question herself about whether she should "put my cat down?"

Linda had been saying to herself, "Do I have to put her out of her suffering?" and this was one of the first questions she had asked Karen.

As Karen continued to talk to the distressed cat an inspired idea came into her mind.

Adya was now three years old and had been spayed long before – and Karen had a sudden feeling that Adya longed for a warm and loving mother-baby relationship! Then she had an idea how this might be brought about and found herself saying emphatically to Linda, "I have a plan! I want you to try something before you make any further decisions. If you will do this, I think it is going to help... "

Linda was open to any suggestion, longing for one in fact, so she listened with interest as Karen suggested that she find Adya an abandoned kitten from the animal shelter, one who was in need of a mother cat, and bring that kitten home and allow Adya to "adopt" the little kitten and bond with it. "She will!" Karen told her.

Linda thought this seemed an impossible recommendation at first, but she was willing to try anything.

So after the session, Linda went back to the animal shelter and asked them whether they had an abandoned kitten who needed a home and a mother, a kitten whom Adya could adopt.

Those who ran the shelter had never been asked such a thing before but were interested in having this possibility tried out. Perhaps, they thought, if this worked, it might start a trend that would save many kittens without mothers and give many mother cats surrogate kittens which might give the adoptive mother cats great comfort and happiness. In this sense, this kitten's adoption would become a test case.

And so, Adya was presented with a little adoptive baby cat who came to her trembling and uncertain and withdrawn. Her heart went out to the little kitten immediately, and despite her own skin disorder, she quickly began to groom the little one, to cuddle her, then to nudge her towards her food and towards sleeping with her all night, her motherly forepaws encircling the kitten. The new plan was working!

Adya became the proud mother of a stray that had been deteriorating, but who now began to flourish under the help and care of a wonderfully devoted mother – and she was the only kitten in the litter, an unusual privilege for a cat!

The little one flourished – and so did Adya. Before the adoption her photos looked, according to Karen, as though she had been "dropped into boiling water" and she was behaving in an extremely disturbed fashion. But the adoption brought about an almost overnight transformation in this cat. So much so, in fact, that the animal shelter later instigated a Surrogate Mother Program for lost kittens which proved to have remarkable results for all concerned.

What this touching success story teaches us is how easy it is to make a mistake when medical authorities look exclusively for the physical causes of behavior and feel they have no recourse but to place the animal on neurological medications such as barbiturates to prevent this sort of self-destructive behavior. The vets are earnestly trying to treat the source of the problem as they see it, but in a situation such as this, treating the more obvious source does not work because the source lies in the past history of the pet itself.

Karen had sensed in a flash that Adya wanted desperately to express her maternal instinct. She felt that if she were this cat she would want to have a kitten lovingly in her care, and It turned out to be so.

Karen feels that instances such as this are the reason why animal communicators must not go just by what the human owner tells them because that person is obviously ignorant of the answer or they would not have consulted them in the first place. The answer, if it can be found, usually lies within the pet itself.

Actually, Karen points out, it is all too easy in today's medically over-sophisticated world with all the information on the Internet, for an owner to become obsessed with the outward symptoms of a pet's illness. Often when they come to Karen, they are almost obsessed with the results of liver counts, potassium counts, CT scans and other objective measurements that constitute a large collection of diagnostic findings. As a result, although the intention of the owner is to help their pet if they possibly can, the animal, responds to their owner's deeper concern (animals can actually feel in their bodies their human's emotions) and can become overwhelmed at that point and not make it through the maze of deep concern, fear, and negative forecasts. At that point, Karen frequently sees a pet begin to fail and give up.

She advises owners that one of the most important things they can do if their pet is seriously ill is to picture that animal as fully recovered. She advises these owners to create a movie in their minds of that animal bouncing around, playing delightedly, barking, or fluttering their wings, or whatever suits their species as a way of expressing a delight in living. The more often the owner can visualize these happy scenes, the more the pet will respond positively to the now changed attitude of the owner. In this sense, owners can be an extraordinary help to their pets because the pets are so exquisitely sensitive to every nuance of their owner's feelings and thoughts. They reverberate with the owner immediately, and the latter's attitude can then be seen reflected in the animal's behavior and state of health.

The Power of Pet Owners to Heal Their Pet

As a pet owner, you can help your animal immensely because they are so closely attuned to your own moods and catch your thoughts so readily. This is a big responsibility that can be used to great advantage if your pet is in distress. Most likely, without you knowing it, you are wordlessly conveying to your pet exactly what you are thinking and feeling and when you begin to send positive messages mentally to them that are different from any former fear of negative consequences that you may have had, something very wonderful can occur..

Karen and I are particularly eager that you get this message while you read this book because all too often, when she is through working with a pet owner and they have discovered the cause of their pet's problem, she finds to her chagrin that the pet owner will at the last moment revert to their original worrying about the outcome of the pet's difficulty. All too often, they will go back to asking about the cause of the disease or its outcome. They are understandably trying to sew up loose ends and be sure they understand what the future may bring. But in doing so they are in inadvertently stirring up the problem again for the animal.

Actually, many people have an obsession with "understanding" what happened and what is likely to happen, rather than allowing themselves to go with the flow of life and feel the joy of a recovery. This obsession with "understanding" at all costs seems to be hard-wired into the human psyche. I often find this in my own work with people whom I see try to sew up the loose ends of every corner of a situation when they would be far better moving into the future with a new, fresh, hopeful attitude. In fact, one of the greatest lessons that animals can teach us is how we can let go of the past and of negative memories and fears and simply drop a situation once we have a solution and move into a happier state.

We cannot emphasize strongly enough that the best way to handle your pet's difficulty, once you understand it, is to envision that animal as happy, healthy, and whole. Even if they only have a limited time left to live, the greatest help you can be to them is to make sure that the time that is left for them is filled with positive, joyful energy at every possible moment. Adya the cat illustrates perfectly how having a reason to get better was all that was needed in her particular case. She now had a baby cat to care for whom she loved, and as soon as this came about, she began to re-grow her hair in the bald spots all over her body where it had been torn out. Quite soon she was able to regrow a beautiful healthy coat of hair. In this case, there was complete healing for all concerned and it came from the power of love.

Karen advises owners not to be afraid of an easy solution if one is found. It doesn't matter how many specialists they may have taken the animal to or how many days and nights they may have agonized over their pet's situation, it can often be healed when the animals point of view is finally seen and understood..

Still Another Effect of Trauma
The Cat Meepers

Meepers had been excessively timid to start with, and like the cat Adya, she too had been separated at far too young an age from her birth mother. As we have seen, often when animals display puzzling behavior, trauma can be the hidden culprit.

Ginny R., a volunteer at a local animal rescue station, owned three cats and consulted Karen about her gray and white tabby named Meepers.

One of the striking things about this case was Ginny's unusually strong devotion to this particular cat whom she had not even known from kittenhood. She described herself as "totally connected" to Meepers for a reason she could not explain.

However, in the two years Ginny had owned her, to Ginny's distress and great inconvenience, she reported that Meepers had never consented to use her litter box!

"No matter what I do," Ginny said, "Meepers always poops outside the litter box!"

Then Ginny cried out, "I don't know what to do! I love this cat. I don't want to rehome this cat. I won't rehome this cat. Please help me!"

When Karen first saw the photo of Meepers she immediately warmed up to this cute little pet whom Karen describes as an "adorable short-haired, gray and white tabby". When she first connected with her at the telephone conference, Meepers wasted no time before telling Karen about her basic problem. She said that she didn't feel she was important in the household where she lived because there were two other cats there and she was the last one to arrive.

Meepers emphasized that she didn't know what her purpose was in being in that household or what she needed to do there. She didn't feel she had any role there.

This cat had come from an animal shelter and had been taken from her littermates and her birth mother at an extremely young age. She therefore had very little loving attention early in life and very little socialization. This was certainly not the nurturing, loving environment that any little being would want to start their life with.

Just as with human Post Traumatic Stress Disorder (PTSD), Meepers suffered from an animal form of PTSD caused by early traumatic experiences. In this case, it involved being taken from her mother far too soon.

Although Ginny's initial complaint had been that Meepers "pooped outside the litter box", and this was the identified reason for the visit, Karen didn't discuss this issue with the cat at all. Instead, she asked her, simply, "What's going on? What's the problem? Tell me what's on your mind."

Karen says that she always gives the animal the opportunity to talk with her first and express their point of view before she directs them toward any problem or issue that the human wants to have addressed. She always lets the animal talk first.

When I heard her say this, I remembered how she did exactly this with my cat Dandy when I consulted her near the end of his life. She insisted on connecting with Dandy first before she heard my story about his difficulty.

During the session with Meepers, Karen told Ginny what the cat had expressed to her, which was "I don't feel I'm important".

"You need to make this cat feel important," she said.

Ginny immediately asked, "What can I do to make her feel important? I love this cat!"

"You have to put her up on a pedestal. Literally. Cats get a sense of power when they're physically on a high perch... Height means confidence. Height is important to cats." Karen explained.

"So put this cat up high. Whenever you're around her, pick her up and put her up high, as high as you can reach. And when you connect with her, really be present. Tell her how much you love her and how important she is to you and why she's with you, tell her you rescued her and you want this to be her forever home."

So, although the initial complaint had been "pooping outside the box", Karen never touched on this issue because there was so much emotional disturbance going on in the cat and she felt it best not to press Meepers for anything more than the discussion they had already had.

The session ended with Ginny appreciative, but uncertain as to what the outcome would be.

Then three months later, Ginny phoned to ask for a follow-up session.

Karen asked, "What's your goal?"

"I just want to check in and see how Meeps is doing. I love this cat. I don't know what the connection is but I'm just so in love with this cat! I'm calling because I want to make sure that she's happy and I'm doing all the right things by her and for her, and if there's anything else I can do to make her happy."

Karen had forgotten about the earlier session because since then she had had so many clients to keep track of that the earlier session was not even in her mind when she again connected with this cat.

Fortunately, however, Meepers came forward to tell Karen how joyful she felt. She described an 180-degree turnaround.

Meepers said that now she felt loved, special, and important in her home, and she knew what her job was there, she knew why she was with this family and with Ginny. In fact, now she knew why everything was the way it was and she said she couldn't be happier. Karen could almost see bubbly, sparkly, joyful, happy faces all around the room as she talked with Meepers on the phone.

Then Ginny added this information, "Karen, you won't believe the change in this cat!"

Ginny then reminded her about the earlier session, which Karen had not remembered, and went on to say, "After we had the session and you told me to put her up on a pedestal, I got a bar stool. Any time that I was around the house and she would come near me, I would put her on top of this bar stool and I would fawn over her and tell her how beautiful she was and how much I love her. I always put her up high now. Whenever I can I pick her up off the ground and put her up high.

"And Karen - it has been three months and she has pooped in the litter box every single time since then!"

Karen couldn't get over the difference in this cat. It was startling and she knew that it wasn't just her work as an animal communicator that had brought about Meepers' transformation. It was the fact that this pet owner had paid attention to what she said and done what she had advised her to do.

Ginny had listened to the messages that Meepers was sending and changed what she herself was doing as a result. She had modified her environment to address what the cat needed instead of locking her in a room, forcing pills down her throat, or re-homing her animal – frequent solutions that people apply in desperation when their pet displays difficult behavior. She had listened carefully to what Meepers had conveyed through Karen, and to Karen's suggestions, and that's all it had taken.

This leads us directly to the topic of how you can communicate with your own pet more effectively and do so in a way that will bring the two of you even closer together. We delve into that in this next chapter.

CHAPTER SEVEN

Communicating With A Pet

The preceding anecdotes illustrate an important component in the way our pets naturally communicate with each other and the way they try to reach us.

Animals think largely in terms of images and although they have adopted some human language because they know that humans can sometimes be best understood in this manner, it is not their natural way of thinking.

Visualizing is probably their main way of communicating as is using scents and tastes to convey various concepts. They tend to broadcast their messages to humans through the sense of vision however because we are not very expert at mentally processing scents and tastes the way another animal might be.

An animal's mental images can sometimes be as cryptic and hard to decipher as a dream. So, when you are attempting to understand a pet's communication that is coming through as an image, you may want to look at it somewhat the way you would view hieroglyphics or the pictorial symbols of the Chinese or some other languages.

Particularly when many images flash into your mind, they may well have a story behind them. It is in finding this story that we can discover the message within the image.

In the same way, animals may receive the images we present to them and literally carry out our wishes in surprising ways when we use images to communicate with them instead of or along with words. Such was the case with Karen's dear horse, Dakota.

Dakota

The animal in question was Karen's horse, Dakota. She belonged to both Karen and her husband and was living in their barn when she began to suffer from severe digestive problems. At first, the pain was mild but soon became so intense that on a particular morning when Karen had gone to the barn to feed the horses, she found Dakota lying on the ground, writhing in pain.

Panicked, Karen ran to her side. She recognized then that the horse had some form of colic and, all too familiar with its more serious symptoms, Karen ran to the nearest phone to call the vet.

After that, trying to help as best she could, Karen threw herself on the ground next to Dakota's head. This was a horse very near to her heart. Almost like a child, Karen found herself begging Dakota not to die.

As Karen connected with Dakota's energy and pled with her to live, she suddenly felt a blast of air on her face that was so sharp it was almost as though she had been smacked in the face. Dakota was in a sense almost shouting to her telepathically, "Go away! Just go away!"

Until then Karen hadn't realized how much her own hysterical behavior was upsetting Dakota. What was happening was that all the panic that she was feeling was being sent directly to the horse adding to its misery.

"Get away!" Dakota cried. "Don't you realize my belly hurts? It hurts so much!! Just go away!"

Karen apologized to Dakota and backed away from the horse as she waited for the vet to arrive

Because of Dakota's critical condition, the horse was admitted to the Intensive Care facility for animals about 25 miles from their home. The outlook was considered bleak and it was not easy to diagnose her condition. After a complete examination and diagnostic tests, the only thing the veterinarians could tell the family was that she had a severe unidentifiable bowel obstruction.

They suggested an ultrasound to determine if it was a tumor or some other kind of mass, and this was performed the next day with rather grim results. There was some kind of hard mass within Dakota's intestines that was described as "about the size of a volleyball". Surgery would have been the only way to remove it, but considering Dakota's age, which was almost 18 years, and since she had a long-standing heart murmur, no veterinarian would agree to operate.

So Dakota's condition continued to deteriorate. Every time Karen visited her, she saw the horse standing more limp in her stall, her head hanging lifelessly, her eyes barely open.

All Karen could do was to send her healing energy every day, as many times as possible. She would picture Dakota again in that stall and repeatedly send her a visual image that came intuitively to Karen. At the same time, she kept telling the horse to "Just poop it out, Dakota! Lift your tail and just poop it out!"

Karen's impression was that Dakota thought this was actually a pretty funny message and she telepathically heard the horse make a feeble attempt to laugh. Karen then showed her, in her mind, a rather grotesque picture of her spraying the inside of the pen with manure, all over the walls like a giant manure fountain.

"Okay, mom, I'll try," Dakota said in what seemed to be a tiny whisper. She had been taken off food for the past five days in an attempt to stop the mass from increasing. This was because that was probably the last option for Dakota. Her heart murmur was too severe to proceed with surgery and according to the doctors the mass had become even harder, as though calcified.

Karen and her husband continued to visit Dakota as often as they could, and each time the situation looked more grim. Finally, they began to prepare for the ultimate decision of permitting euthanasia. They were realizing that it was grossly unfair to let her stand there and suffer, she should not be allowed to be in that much pain.

Karen and Dan then decided to visit her one last time and give their authorization for euthanasia. The night before they went to the medical center to do this, Karen prayed almost all night for their horse and again told Dakota over and over telepathically to just get rid of that impaction as though she was painting the stall with manure. The horse's response was barely audible: "I send you both my love." she seemed to say.

Karen was setting out to go to the animal hospital the next day when she received a phone call from the head veterinarian. He was a bit hesitant as he spoke and Karen assumed he had more bad news when he said: "I don't know how to tell you this Karen." But then he went on to say, "I went to check on Dakota and when I looked inside her stall there was manure everywhere there. It was all over the walls! Then I examined her and – the obstruction was gone. I really don't know what to say except that none of us can feel any obstruction at all on palpitation. So we don't see any point in keeping her here. She can go home."

Karen had told Dakota to spray the walls of the stall like a giant manure fountain, using a vivid mental image to reinforce her words, and she had done exactly what her "mom" has asked her to!

Dakota came home after that and soon was a fine, healthy horse and remained so from that time on. The massive ball had been identified as a giant food obstruction that had hardened in her intestines. The combination of fluid she was receiving and Dakota's willingness to "paint the walls of her stall" had led to a full recovery. She had listened to the advice.

Actually, the last thing an animal wants from its beloved owner is to have the person upset by their condition. It is hard for us to realize that because we think that being upset is necessary in order to express our love, and while indeed it is natural to feel this way, it can be very undermining to the pet.

Dakota's reaction to her owner, who happened to be Karen, when Karen broke down when her horse became seemingly terminally ill, is an example of the distrust an animal can feel when it's owner is massively upset at what is happening. Dakota quite clearly told this to Karen when Karen broke down over her upset about her horse's condition.

When Dakota cried out, "Get away from me! You're killing me with your constant fears and upset!" Karen learned an important lesson then and she cannot emphasize enough to her clients (nor can I from what I know of human reactions) how important it is to hold your pet in a positive light, and as much as is humanly possible to experience joy and lightness, regardless of whether the pet can physically or emotionally follow you there right at the moment.

I suggest you use the "Energy Psychology" exercises in Part Two of this book to bring you into this positive mood, which is one of the most effective ways you can possibly express your love for your pet. There you can also learn ways to use other images to communicate with animals:

CHAPTER EIGHT

What Our Pets Know About Us

Animals are incredibly sensitive to the moods and feelings of their special humans and tell us that they feel them in their own bodies. The pet is watching over everything that the human does and they sense many things that the person is feeling, even though they may not understand the reasons for them. People are always looking for reasons, animals do so much less. They simply want to know how to best deal with what's happening. They really only seek to know whether this special person (or persons) of theirs is happy or not and if they seem to be upset, they want this fixed now.

Pets can easily become upset if the human they consider their "parent" is depressed, anxious or otherwise upset as we have seen in the case of Dakota the horse who yelled at Karen "Get away from me!" when Karen was expressing her upset with Dakota's condition. This fact is behind many of the animal disturbances that we hear reported. A good portion of the clients who come to any animal communicator are pets who are actually taking on the pains and distress of a close human being. It is only when we deal with the owner of such a pet and find out what's going on with them and work on clearing it up that the behavior of the animal begins to change.

This is not a very well known fact, but it is an extremely important one when trying to understand where your own pet is coming from emotionally, as the following accounts show.

As it happens, the fact that animals are so sensitive to human emotion has both its good and bad sides. I've just mentioned the way in which animals can sensitively identify with human emotions and often be of immense comfort to the human because of this, but there is another aspect to this ability of the animal to know what is going on with you which can be a detriment if you happen to have some things about you that you would rather not have known to others.

Secrets Your Pets May Know

Below we tell you what can happen if you have a secret you want to conceal for one reason or another and your pet knows it. Their inherent honesty and directness will not permit them to hide any information they know about you if they are asked about it by anyone they are willing to communicate with. Perhaps in this respect, it is a blessing that most humans cannot converse with animals and so it is not possible to pick their brains with regard to family secrets. The frequent human need to conceal information or misrepresent it by telling what we call a "lie" is something your pet doesn't understand or recognize. If you have something you want to keep under cover when you are consulting with an animal communicator don't expect your pet to recognize this need.

During the days when Karen was a deputy police officer she was particularly impressed by how, to the inconvenience of their owners, certain pets were able to reveal who was the real culprit in domestic violence police investigations.

We have mentioned the time a small herd of deer directed Karen to a suspect concealed in the woods when she was a police officer. This is only one of many instances where an animal's extreme sensitivity led to finding the culprit where there had been misbehavior. Presumably, this is because animals are unaware of the legal consequences of telling the truth. Karen points out that animals will either answer with the truth when we ask them a simple cause and effect question or if they are afraid of you, they will not answer at all. When they answer with information the person has concealed from authorities they do this because truth is their only reality although unfortunately, it may not seem this way to the human involved.

Because of their truthful behavior, born of their innocence and nonjudgmental nature, Karen found that pets in a home where there had been some kind of violence would quite innocently identify the culprit even if this person was someone they dearly loved. Since they do not experience blame no matter what– although they can fear the perpetrator of a crime and want to protect their human against him or her – they seem to see no reason not to answer questions put to them by a friendly person such as Karen, by telling the truth and they had no inkling that any bad consequences might stem from doing so.

Angelina Reveals an Embarrassing Secret

In her present role of animal communicator, Karen tells an amusing story of a time that she innocently asked a question of an animal whom she was trying to assist. This happened when the animal's owner consulted her about her beautiful tabby cat, who answered with complete candor a question Karen asked her, much to the embarrassment of her owner.

The cat, Angelina, was brought to Karen's attention because she was engaging in behavior that was extremely upsetting to her owner. The owner had a hobby of collecting very fine designer shoes and for the past several months this cat had developed the habit of foraging in her owner's shoe closet and finding her most cherished and expensive shoes and seemingly intentionally peeing on them. She was ruining pair after pair of her "mother's" prized collection this way.

When Karen made friends with the cat and began to talk with her, she finally asked Angelina why she was damaging her "mother's" best shoes. The cat told her immediately that it was because she was mad at her owner "mother" because she had not let her into her bedroom at a time when Angela had asked, by mewing persistently, to enter it.

Karen wanted to learn a little more about this incident and as they talked she explained to Angelina that at certain times people might not want their pets in their bedrooms for reasons that had nothing whatsoever to do with whether the mommy or daddy loved their pet. Perhaps, she said, her mommy and daddy were simply busy doing other things at that time.

Angelina immediately clarified the situation by saying, "But the man in that room wasn't my Daddy."

Since, as a professional, Karen had been consulted about the cat's shoe destroying behavior, she felt she had no alternative but to repeat this message to the owner, and did so. Whereupon the woman became outraged that Karen "could suggest such a thing!" and abruptly terminated the phone call without saying goodbye. Karen never heard from her again and presumably the attacks on the shoes continued.

This is an example of the way in which our animals observe us minutely in ways we have no idea they are doing. This cat had not in any way indicated that she thought her mother's behavior to be "wrong" in any moral sense, as a person might– animals don't judge that way – she had just said it made her feel "very mad" to be shut out of the room when she had asked so clearly to be admitted and that she was peeing on her mother's favorite shoes to show her objection.

Pets' Behaviors During Police Investigations

Many times when Karen was serving as a deputy and was assigned to a domestic violence case, she had a chance to converse with the pets of the persons being investigated. When she did so these animals would often innocently report serious matters such as who had struck whom and under what circumstances, and clearly had no awareness that they might be incriminating those people they loved by telling the truth.

Since a pet's testimony does not hold up in court (a gross understatement I might add!) Karen didn't report what they told her to the police force, but she did listen with seriousness to these reports, and they often helped her considerably in determining who the culprit was in a domestic struggle and where to investigate next to solve the case.

Why, you may ask, did these animals so readily reveal what could be incriminating evidence regarding owners they so loved?

The answer seems to lie in the completely nonjudgmental nature of pets. They are not blaming their human for anything they do because blame is not in their vocabulary – they don't know what it is. The pet is simply observing and telling the truth because they do not have a mindset that includes blame. They do not realize that other parties or the police might be condemning their owner and that the truth might get the owner in a great deal of trouble. The concept of blame doesn't jive with the animal's love for those to whom they are loyal.

Two Siamese Cats Help Catch a Murderer

Probably the most striking instance of this kind of loyalty has to do with a murder that Karen was asked to help with when a former client who had consulted Karen with regard to one of her pets, called her to tell her that her brother had been murdered almost 10 years before and that the case had been closed for the past 3 years due to the fact that the body was never recovered. One cannot arrest a suspect if a body is not found, and eventually the entire case had been abandoned.

However, the lingering effect on the family was still a very painful one, and as it happened, the victim had had two Siamese cats he was extremely fond of who had been found at the scene of the murder and Karen's client Catherine had adopted these cats after her brother's death and they still lived with her, happily it seemed. Catherine asked Karen whether she (Karen) could question the two cats about what had happened at the time of the murder because they had been found there hiding under the bed and must have witnessed the struggle. Karen simply replied that she would try.

Because she prefers to introduce her conversations with animals on a reassuring note and not make them into a formal interrogation when she connected with these two cats, she simply said casually to the cats, "Hey, what happened to your dad?", after they had been conversing for a little while.

The cats then described a scene of many struggles, as they had seen it from beneath the bed where they were hiding. They said that two men had come into the room and they had recognized one of them by his shoes. This man had on work boots while the other man was wearing tennis shoes. One of the cats then described "a big fight where there was a lot of screaming." and said it had been "horrible".

"They took our dad away and he never came back." one cat told her. As it finally turned out through investigation, they had taken the body to another state and dumped it.

Karen asked if this cat knew the name of the man who had been familiar to them and the pet answered by giving her three initials "A.R.J." Interestingly, when Karen told these initials to Catherine, the latter told her that the prime suspect had been a man by the name of "Arnold Rogers, Junior", obviously he had had the initials "A.R.J." When Karen asked this cat where his dad had been taken, the cat simply said, cryptically, the numbers "1515" and the words "two spoons".

These were insufficient clues to allow anyone to solve the case and Catherine soon abandoned her effort to do so, and Karen did not hear from her for two years. However, after that much time had elapsed, Catherine finally contacted Karen again to tell her that her brother's body had eventually been found at an address which was "1515 Two Spoons Road" in a neighboring state where a farmer had discovered the deteriorating remains when plowing his field.

At that point, Catherine, obviously impressed with the information Karen had given her about the address, asked whether Karen could now contact her brother directly, the one who had been murdered, on the "other side" the way she could contact departed animals. Karen said she thought she could and would try but wasn't sure, but in fact, she had very little difficulty connecting with Catherine's brother when she finally did arrange to do so. He seemed eager to make a connection with his family and "came in quickly" when she contacted him.

In answer to Karen's questions, all he had to say about his murder was that it was "a drug deal gone bad" and went on to say that he loved his big Siamese cats and was extremely glad that his sister had taken them in and was giving them such great care. He seemed much more interested in telling the family that he was okay then to talk about the murder. In response to questioning about the latter, all he was willing to say was that the two men had beat him up very badly before they killed him, but he didn't want to talk about any of the details.

He seemed to want to use his energy to talk about how well he was now, 12 years later, and to reassure the family of this.

Because it was too late to apprehend the suspects and the body had deteriorated seriously, this murder was never officially "solved", but Karen's interviews did yield some useful information for the family.

When a Crucial Animal Message Could Never Be Revealed

Karen remembers another case where a woman was missing in a very rough rocky terrain near the shore and the police report attributed her disappearance as being due to a "rogue wave" that suddenly washed up on the beach and dragged her away. This was during the time that Karen was a deputy and she had been assigned to the case.

The woman's two dogs had been found running distractedly up and down the beach near where she had been lost, and when these dogs were questioned by Karen they described something quite different from the story which the official police report offered. The dogs told Karen that a man had "taken her away" in a truck. At that time, the police had not leaked out the information that there had been two other abductions in that area in recent weeks.

After Karen spoke to the dogs and found out what they had to say about the man taking her off in a truck, she tried to contact the woman's family directly, but when the family did not want to speak to her, she abandoned this effort. Had she continued the investigation, this would have been considered interfering in a crime. Unless you are invited to do so, such behavior is not legal for a police officer.

I report these accounts of animals who witnessed crimes and were able to talk about them afterwards, revealing details, to illustrate the manner in which animals observe their owners in the greatest detail at all times and once again to emphasize the fact that they do not experience blame, although clearly, an animal will defend their owner against an attack even with their own life, if necessary. The instinct to protect its human family is tremendous, as has been noted throughout history.

In the next chapter, we will be looking at the equally strong protection which a human can feel toward their pet. If a person thinks they have not taken adequate care of their pet, they can become deeply distressed and even seriously depressed. Many times this distress is entirely unnecessary, but the person does not realize this.

CHAPTER NINE

Humans Riddled With Guilt

Sometimes unfortunate things happen to their beloved pet that can leave pet owners overwhelmed with a feeling of guilt. This is far more common a response to a pet's illness or death, for example, than is generally realized and one of the most frequent reasons why people consult animal communicators. They long for reassurance that they are not responsible for unfortunate things that have happened to their pet.

All too frequently, however, no reassurance, including positive reports from the animals themselves completely exonerating their owners whom they dearly love, will do any good even though the owner is the one who has sought out the communicator. The self-recrimination following harm to a pet for which the owner often feels unnecessarily responsible can persist for a long time and require much treatment before it dissipates. If you find yourself in such a situation we suggest you consult the exercises that address this problem in Part Two of this book.

Guilt is an especially difficult emotion to overcome because the self-blame brought about by it can be so persistent or can even last for a lifetime. The following stories show how Karen has dealt with humans who were experiencing extreme guilt with regard to their beloved animals. Such guilt was totally unnecessary in these cases but the human did not know this.

The Tragic Death of a Teacup Poodle

One day Karen received a call from a distraught woman regarding her miniature poodle who had died as a result of an accident she herself had actually caused. She and her husband had been driving home with their dog in the back of the car. Both had been drinking and they were arguing intensely during the drive home. When they arrived and were getting out of the car, they each thought the other one had grabbed the dog.

The result of their confusion was that when the

woman got out of the car and slammed the door, still intensely angry from the argument, she accidentally caught the dog's head in the car door as the latter started to jump out. This resulted in a horrible and eventually fatal accident. While the injury didn't kill the dog immediately, it was so severely wounded that it had to be euthanized, adding to the trauma surrounding this incident.

The woman was upset to the extreme because she was riddled with guilt. She was so distraught, in fact, she could barely tell Karen what happened when she first contacted her over the telephone.

When she phoned her for the actual session, Karen quickly connected to the little dog's energy and the little euthanized dog came to her in spirit quickly.

The fact was that this poodle was just as happy as could be!

"Tell Mom I'm here!" the dog said cheerfully "Tell her I'm fine. Tell her I love her." and then the dog went on to enthusiastically describe all the things you would expect to hear from a dog that had a great life and great family and people who loved it.

This information made almost no impression upon the distraught owner, however. She simply could not forgive herself and kept compulsively blaming herself, almost in the same words, over and over again. She had thought her husband had the dog; he had thought she had the dog. They were fighting and intoxicated and shouldn't have had the dog with them and this was an ugly situation.

Nonetheless, Karen had been contacted by the owner to find out what condition the little dog was in now and actually she found out almost immediately that the dog was in a condition that could almost be described as an "ideal" state. The little dog had no bad feelings toward either of her owners and wanted them to share in its present excitement. It did not feel like talking to Karen about any details of the accident other than that it had felt extreme pressure when the door slammed on its head, it wanted to go on to talk about the good things it was experiencing now.

Aside from remembering feeling the pressure, the dog actually had no memory whatsoever of anything else that happened after the blow. In fact, anything that occurred immediately after that accident took place held no interest for the dog.

The woman, however, was so distraught that Karen had to schedule many sessions with her before the latter began to understand that her little dog was now actually fine, didn't hold anything against her, and was experiencing no bad repercussions from the accident.

Although Karen told this owner repeatedly that her beloved dog, in spirit, was doing fine and loved her just as much as she did him right now, the woman could not seem to hear what Karen was saying. Her emotions were so raw that in fact for a long time she was barely able to function in daily life. She couldn't work, she could barely sleep and was almost completely incapacitated. It took more than a year of counseling with Karen for her to work through the emotional devastation this accident had caused and it was only after much time had passed and countless attempts to clarify this on the part of Karen, that the woman began to understand the amazing fact that the little dog was happy, loved her and did not even need to forgive her because he (the dog) felt no blame whatsoever.

This startling fact with respect to total forgiveness is a great lesson for us humans although many people are unable to benefit from that lesson because they cannot even conceive of the extent of an animal's unconditional love.

A Lethal Dose of Medicine

Another tragic incident involved the accidental death of a cat because of an inadvertent administration of a lethal dose of a medicine.

The owner of the cat phoned Karen originally because she had given her cat ibuprofen, not knowing that Ibuprofen will kill a cat. She had thought she was doing the right thing in giving her cat this medicine because the animal was having issues with pain. Tragically, this owner ended up poisoning her cat.

In this particular situation, the cat was initially not lethally ill before receiving the drug and just needed to go to the vet. Karen's client was trying to medicate it herself, however, both to relieve the cat's pain and save herself the cost of a visit to the vet.

Sadly, she ended up losing her very dear pet.

When Karen connected with the cat telepathically at the owner's request, it showed great excitement at connecting with its "Mom" and wanted to share adventurous stories and talk about the things she and her mom had done during its lifetime as well as things that were currently going on. But all that Karen's client wanted to talk about was the horrible struggle and painful death she remembered her cat experiencing.

In truth, this client was talking about her own memory of what had happened, not the cat's recall of it. Her own memory was very painful, and her guilt very deep. Guilt is one of the worst feelings people can possibly experience because it can cause bitter self-recrimination.

Some Tips for the Guilt Ridden

As we have seen, animals, both here on earth and spiritually in the afterlife, pick-up on the emotions of the humans they love and are deeply affected by them. They actually feel those emotions in their own bodies. Whatever the emotion is that their humans are experiencing, the animal feels it.

According to Karen, this means that if you are ruminating on and visualizing a tragic event involving your pet over and over again, that animal, whether they're alive or have passed on, will pick up on everything you're thinking. They know that the thoughts in your mind are about them and therefore they know that you feel horrible as you think about them. This means that the message they are getting is, "My human thinks about me and feels horrible!"

In their simplistic world, the animal puts those two things together and usually arrives at the conclusion: "I'm making my person feel horrible."

To pet owners who may be experiencing guilt about real or imagined things they did that they believe were harmful to their animal, we give the following advice.

Rather than dwell on those painful thoughts of self-recrimination you can help your pet far more by understanding how your loved animal actually wants you to be joyful and to live fully in each moment. Realize that the animal can't understand why you would want to worry about the past. It also can't understand why you would want to worry about the future. Animals don't recognize or in any way understand our human feelings about the passage of time and the importance of times other than the present. It is actually a meaningless concept to them.

And if your pet has passed on and they no longer have a physical body but are pure energy, it is as though they had gotten rid of all the static of having a body so that now they are getting pure messages, not garbled ones. The images that come to them are very clear now, very precise, and as we have been emphasizing in this book, they are able to immediately absorb and respond to whatever you are feeling.

If the animal loved you, after they pass on they're going to stay close to you and thus they will be picking up on your emotions at all times – right now in fact. That's why it's so important to the healing process that if you feel sadness or you feel bad about something else relating to your pet, for your pet's sake as well as your own, much the best thing you can do is try to think of something positive that has to do with your animal, something that would bring a smile to your face. Or recall a happy memory that you have of your departed animal so that this can help both you and the one that has transitioned. To allow your earthly relationship with your pet to end on a positive note in your own mind is the best choice you can possibly make.

When Karen has to spend time counseling a pet owner who is guilt-ridden, she explains to them that your depressed mood and very strong negative feelings can prevent this animal from continuing on their spirit journey, which they need to do because they continue to learn and grow on the other side.

Animals, she tells us, have things they need to do. There is soul growth for animals just as there is soul growth for humans, even though it is a little bit different than that which humans experience. Karen has found over the years that if a person finally realizes that they are holding their animal back and causing them to be stuck, by holding on to negative feelings and guilt, this often brings about a basic change in the way they feel about the whole situation, and both owner and pet can now move forward constructively.

CHAPTER TEN

Lost Animals

One of the most devastating experiences pet owners face is having their pet lost and unable to be located. They do not know where to find them, whether they are safely being cared for by some adoptive humans that are kind, whether they are in grave danger for their life or whether they will ever see them again. They do not even know if they are still alive. This is often as frightening and painful an experience as it would be if a child were kidnapped.

Animal Communicators are contacted very frequently for help in locating a lost pet and it is one of the most difficult problems for them to solve because the animal cannot tell them exactly where they are but simply send mental images of being under a bush, in a forest, beneath a porch or in some other general vicinity, but who knows where that vicinity is actually located geographically – there is no telling where that bush or under what porch or by what river it is located.

Owners often become desperate when their initial search turns up no leads and days or weeks go by when there is no trace of the animal. Not knowing what is happening to their beloved pet is the most unbearable part of the experience.

Also, there are distinct species differences in the behavior of lost animals. Lost dogs behave very differently from lost cats, for example, and it is important for pet owners to know what these differences are.

Lost felines will go into effective survival mode very quickly when separated from their families. They begin slinking around and show great cautiousness and a helpfully suspicious attitude. They will be keenly aware of any possible danger in their surroundings, and be extra careful to ensure that nothing in their proximity will attack or harm them.

It doesn't take very long for lost cats to become feral, reverting to their instinctive wild state. In survival mode, their bodies automatically begin conserving calories and energy. Typically, they tend to hide, and to watch and wait during the day until the most quiet times of dawn and dusk to emerge and seek nourishment.

Dogs, on the other hand, act very differently. Their response to being lost is often to run, and run - and run, often traveling great distances from home. They can be found 50 or 100 miles away from where they have lived, something rare for a cat. Also, dogs aren't as adept as cats, in general, when it comes to survival skills. While a few dogs will hunker down and hide, most lost canines will simply run aimlessly, often into unsafe areas such as busy streets where they can easily be hit by a car.

Because they are excellent hunters, when they are lost cats can be extremely resourceful at finding food versus dogs, which are typically scavengers, seeking edible things that someone has left behind. Because of these distinct species differences, when Karen receives a call regarding a lost cat, she often directs the pet owner to search very near the last place that they saw the cat because most lost cats are found within a mile or less from home.

In lost dog cases, she tells pet owners to search farther and farther away from the last place that they saw the dog because lost dogs can just keep running until they become exhausted and run out of energy. When that happens, they may find a place to hide or wander to someone's house seeking food and human contact.

When lost pets do seek and find humans who will shelter them, sometimes the humans will not try to find the animal's owner at all but will claim the pet as their own. Such was the case in the following story.

Charlie is Missing!

One summer, Karen received a call about a missing six-year-old Shih Tzu/Yorkie mixed breed dog, Charlie. This dog's owner, Anna, had taken Charlie with her on a visit to her sister's house in Wyoming during the

Fourth of July weekend. On the evening of July 3, Anna and her sister put Charlie in the fenced back yard and went to the movies.

Although it was the season of fireworks, Anna, didn't think twice about this fact because fireworks were prohibited in her community. Unfortunately, they were legal where her sister lives and that evening the neighborhood resounded with firework explosions. When the sisters returned home, Charlie had disappeared. Terrified of the fireworks, the tiny dog had managed to scale the 4-foot chain-linked fence and run away!

After two days of searching for little Charlie, Anna recalled reading an article about Karen in the local newspaper and decided to contact her. Although Anna had never dealt with an animal communicator before, she and her two young, heartbroken children were desperate to try anything to find their precious dog.

Karen immediately prepared to communicate with Charlie telepathically and the first image he sent her was of him on something soft, like carpet, along with vivid images of a pond and floating ducks. She also sensed in her body his fear and desire to go home. In more images, Charlie showed Karen that he was presently restrained by being tied up, but the other images he was sending were confusing.

Karen told Anna about the images Charlie had sent her.

"Oh yes, I bring Charlie to a nearby pond where he loves barking at the ducks," Anna said in a sad voice, "We did go by that park during our search, hoping he had somehow made it back there to find his ducks, but there was no Charlie." Anna was fighting back her tears.

Karen often receives messages from lost animals that are confusing. Both the emotions of the humans and the lost animal can interfere with Karen's reception, similar to the way a microwave oven will interfere with a cordless phone making the transmission broken and raspy. In this case, Karen could not determine if Charlie was even still alive. They would have to wait to see if someone found him, or wait for other images that he might send to Karen.

Out of understandable frustration, Anna then contacted another psychic for assistance. The psychic claimed that raccoons had attacked and killed Charlie and that he had crossed over to the spirit world. To confirm her little dog's demise, Anna contacted Karen again.

However, Karen did not feel that Charlie had died. While his previous messages were confusing, she could still feel the energy of his physical body when she connected telepathically with him. So she again connected with Charlie and this time his messages were extremely clear. He showed Karen a public restroom in a campground. There was a statue. So Karen told Anna to seek out the campground as described and the statue. She said that if Anna stood in front of the statue and looked up, she would see where Charlie was being held captive.

From the images that Charlie was flashing to Karen, she was also able to describe to Anna a panoramic view of where he was from his perspective. It was about a mile from her sister's house. Karen also saw the woman who had taken Charlie in. This woman had some sort of disability that caused her to limp, she was in her mid to late forties, and had shoulder-length graying brown hair. Karen sensed that the woman's energy was one of irrationality and that she was difficult to deal with.

Additionally, Karen was able to describe the woman's house, the vehicles in the driveway, and other buildings behind and around the home. She told Anna that there seemed to be lots of activity around the property, along with a great deal of negative energy enveloping it.

With this new information, Anna set out to find her beloved Charlie and shortly thereafter, both Anna and Karen believed he had been located. However, actually getting Charlie back became quite a challenge.

Upon escaping from her sister's house, he had ended up at some rodeo grounds about a mile away. On the grounds, there was a public restroom and a bucking bronco statue (quite close to the truth as they later discovered, Karen had deciphered Charlie's imagery as a "campground"). When Anna found the rodeo grounds, she stood at the statue, looked up, and there along the tree line she saw the woman's house that Karen had described to her. From the color of the house to the type of vehicle in the driveway, and the surrounding buildings, Karen's details were nearly exact. Anna contacted the police and filed a report with all of the essential information.

The woman Karen had described lived with her husband and teenage children. The local police had suspicions that there was drug activity there and when they first visited to talk to the woman, who was, as Karen described, in her mid to late forties with graying brown, shoulder-length hair, she was indeed argumentative, irrational, and uncooperative.

Still determined, Anna posted flyers seeking help in her attempt to regain her dog and even mailed them to pet-related businesses in the area. Then one day, she received a phone call from a local pet groomer who had received one of the flyers. The groomer told Anna that a woman had come in with a dog that looked like Charlie. The groomer had informed this woman that he didn't have any open times that day and had scheduled her for a day later in the week. After gathering the woman's contact information, he promptly called Anna, who immediately contacted the police again.

During several visits by the police to the woman's house, the family insisted they did not have a dog. On one occasion, they told the police that the woman who had the dog had moved away. In disbelief, the police decided to show up unannounced on another day and there was Charlie on the front porch!

Charlie's ordeal lasted nearly four weeks and without Anna's determination, he might never have been found. When Charlie reunited with Anna, he was wearing his old collar and had an ear infection, but overall was in good health.

Now Karen recounts a case with characteristics that are generally uncommon in most lost cat cases.

Finding Milo

One spring day, Karen received a call from a woman, Tami, who lives in a small Virginia farming town. She was calling about her lost cat, Milo. Shortly after Milo's disappearance from her rural home, Tami knew something was amiss because Milo ordinarily never traveled farther than their barn. When he hadn't come home for his dinner a few nights before and didn't return after that, she decided to reach out to Karen.

Milo was a beautiful, solidly black cat whom Karen connected with almost immediately. The cat showed Karen what seemed to be a large snow-covered area, and when Karen told Tami what she was seeing, Tami laughed and explained that they lived among cotton fields. They had just harvested and the fields were covered in blankets of white cotton!

As Milo continued to show Karen images, she knew he was definitely on the move. He was flashing her images of barns, tractors, cows, silos, farm trucks, and farmers in their overalls. And on her part, Tami would seek Karen from various locations near her farm to see if she could find anything matching these images.

Several weeks passed with no sign of Milo but whenever Karen checked in with him, he sent her messages that he was alive, fine, and a bit "plump." He was having no trouble finding food.

When lost cats revert to survival mode, they can become very skittish and may not even respond to calls from their human family. As Milo continued to show Karen images of farmhouses, outbuildings, and piles of bricks, she knew this was not a typical lost cat – this cat was on a mission!

For nine long weeks of searching, Tami encountered countless black cat sightings and dead-end leads, and she was becoming extremely frustrated and frayed. When Tami did spot a black cat, most would scurry off before she could get close. With Milo having no collar and no other markings, identifying him from a distance would be nearly impossible.

So Tami decided to ask Karen to check in with Milo one more time and this time the images Milo showed Karen were very different from those he had relayed to her previously. She now saw white houses with green trim, a triangular area that appeared to be a park or ball field, and some "pink things" in manicured grass. Karen then sought some spiritual guidance in hope of determining how far away Milo was from home. Suddenly, the number fifteen came to her, as in fifteen miles, which was much farther away than the area in which Tami had been searching.

Tami was on the verge of giving up when she suddenly received a phone call from the woman who had moved into her former home. The woman asked, "Hey, are you missing Milo? He just walked into the barn and began eating my cat's food like he owned the place!"

"Yes, I'm missing Milo!" Tami yelled. "Is it really him?"

"I think so." the woman replied. "He's a bit chubby."

Tami drove the fifteen miles as fast as she could to her old house and barn. Actually, if Milo had made a beeline back to his old barn from the new barn, it would have only been about an eight-mile jaunt. Milo chose the scenic route, meandering across fields and pastures!

As Tami arrived at the house, she passed a triangular ball field with manicured grass not far from the barn. Once in the driveway, Tami saw that the house had now been painted white with green trim and there were pink brightly colored toys lying all around the yard!

She thought to herself, "Milo sent these very images to me with Karen's help!" She was truly amazed and quickly ran to the barn, where she picked up her chubby black Milo, giving him the biggest hug that she could!

Since Tami reunited with Milo and brought him home, she will not allow him to go outdoors unless she is home to keep watch over him. Milo is also now sporting a bright, lime-green colored collar -- and in that small Virginia farming community, all black cats no longer look the same!

In the next chapter, Karen and some other animal communicators will answer questions that may be accumulating in your mind. You will see the answers in this next chapter.

CHAPTER ELEVEN

Questions For Animal Communicators

Here are some of the questions most frequently asked of Animal Communicators

How did my pet die? Did it suffer?

Often pet owners want Karen to find out exactly how their pet died if they weren't there when it did. They want to know if it was taken by a predator, let's say a lost animal, or if it was hit by a car or whatever the cause. They then all too often want to know what Karen calls "all the gory details about what happened".

Karen points out that for the animal when she contacts them, that is the last thing they want to discuss. In fact, some departed pets directly refuse to share this information with her at all. When this happens, she honors that and never tries to obtain information from an animal that they clearly don't want to share. As she says, "Typically, pets just don't see the point of going over the worst moment of their existence and rehashing it, they are simply not interested in remembering the blood and gore, the pain and the distress of it all. They have moved on from that."

If the owner is inquiring about the cause of death, at this point, she says, she has to try to look at the situation objectively to determine what happened – was it, for example, due to an accident or were they taken by a predator? She points out that an animal's experience is typically simple and brief surrounding how they actually ended their life if either of these things happens. They are apt to say something to her when she asks, such as, "I don't know. Something just came up behind me. I don't know what it was."

About this she comments rather humorously "It's not like they turn around, look at their attacker and say: 'Oh, hi, what's your name?" Rather, if they were attacked, the end was often sudden and very quick. They're here one second and they're gone the next second. They don't dwell on it at all. It's not something that they can dredge up in their memory to please us humans later because they simply don't hold onto those memories."

"The animals tell me that it actually brings them down emotionally and actually makes them feel like they're doing something wrong, to talk about their death or how they died. "

Karen explains to her clients that the death experience, and whatever trauma their pet may have had around it, is usually briefly gone through. If the death is an accident or has occurred in the wild, it is often not even in their memory banks anymore. It has been erased, and for her to try to dredge it up, in her words, "really doesn't do anybody any good." She points out that if you notice, or have ever read about a horrific car accident, for example, the person involved will often have no memory of the accident itself, none. Nature often takes care of such things by bringing on amnesia.

The fact is that it is probably as likely that the animal felt practically no experience of pain at the moment of an attack by a predator than it is that they suffered. This is due to the body's protective chemicals that can anesthetize pain. It is also probable that if they did experience great pain because they were killed by a predator, that this was usually very brief because the predator is programmed to know exactly how to bring about a very rapid death in their prey, without struggle.

Karen keeps emphasizing that animals do not dwell on the past as people are so apt to do. If the situation has been corrected and they are no longer in distress the animal usually wants to drop the memory and live happily in the present.

This is a lesson for those who adopt rescue animals – animals who have been mistreated or neglected by previous owners and were often subjected to serious adverse circumstances in the past. It is a wonderful thing to be able to adopt a rescue animal and bring joy to the life of an animal that would have been tragically damaged had they not been brought into a shelter and given out for adoption.

However once this has been done, they must be allowed to build a new life for themselves without being reminded of their past unfortunate experiences and the most helpful thing you can do for your rescue animal is to deemphasize the fact that they were ever mistreated. While your natural inclination may be to tell people you meet about your animal's tragic past because you are so concerned with trying to help the animal overcome that past, the fact is that repeating the unhappy story will only pull the animal down because they will understand an incredible amount of what you are saying. Now that the rescue animal has begun a new life the best thing you can do for them is to imagine as delightful a future for them as possible and not dwell on the fact that they were rescued from a deeply disturbing situation.

What rescue animals need most is to be able to bound into the future with joy, and it can be extremely helpful to them if, as the owner of a rescue animal, you gloss over their unfortunate past as quickly as possible by saying something like, "actually he (or she) was a rescue animal but presently they have a wonderful happy life, good food and lots of love and they love playing with my grandchildren etc." You can't emphasize the positive enough and by not going into the story of their past unhappiness you are helping the animal to forget those incidents, which is their natural instinct to do. Animals have an enviable ability to live in the present and move into the future with excitement and joy. In this respect, they can be great teachers for us.

Will my pet go to heaven?

Here I report to you what Karen has experienced hundreds of times with respect to that question. When animals transition from the earth and Karen connects with their spirit energies and the God Source or "creator source", she sees what she calls a "hierarchy" within that energy.

In describing it she asks us to picture the center of all things, and at the core of that, to envision the Creator, however, you may view this divine source. According to Karen's often repeated vision, you have, next to the Creator itself, animals and archangels. She says that she sees them as right there next to the Creator. Then, moving out from the circle, she sees the Masters such as Christ or Buddha and other very highly evolved souls. Out much further from the center, she sees people "like you and me, we are way out there," she says.

Karen feels strongly that when animals pass away they go straight to the Source more easily than we do. "They go right to the Creator because they are pure love," she says.

I do not pretend to know myself what happens, but I know that numerous animal communicators have reported the experience of the afterlife as described by departed animals whom they contact, to be one of joy and wonder - very close indeed to our traditional vision of heaven.

Does my departed pet miss me?

This is one of the questions that is most frequently asked of animal communicators and Karen tells me that she always has difficulty telling them the seemingly disappointing news that: "No, they don't miss you in the way you miss them. It's not that way for them. We miss that warm body to cuddle. We miss seeing them in all their favorite places. We miss that physical animal there to pet and love. That's what we miss. That's not what animals experience."

But while they never say that they "miss" their owners this seems largely to be due to the fact that they spend inordinate amounts of time with their owners after they pass. Animals frequently tell Karen that they now have more continuous contact with their special human than they did when they were living. They often describe being with their human 24/7 and traveling with them wherever they go. They tell us that they love it that they can now be around their human day and night, as much as they want. They can go places with them that they were never allowed to go before, places that they were not free to go when they were here on earth.

The animals, therefore, don't seem to miss us the way we miss them because they say they often get more of us than they ever got when on earth. They don't have a physical body, so they don't need that physical contact, and because they seem to be made of love, they actually live off of our loving energy. What they crave is our love, and for us to be happy and joyous. When we are sad, depressed, upset, angry, guilty, or hurt, or experiencing any other negative emotions, as Karen puts it, "They come down with us."

We cannot repeat too often that when a person is extremely upset it is important for that person to realize that it is not just themselves who are experiencing that emotion, but they are sending it out to everyone who loves them and cares about them, especially when these people or animals are on the "other side". "Departed spirits can pick up on their loved ones' emotions immediately, the animal communicators tell us, and the human's energy can actually make them feel either wonderful or very sad.

If "their person" is having a really hard time with losing their pet, the animal will tell the animal communicator that this is dragging them (the pet) down. Karen reports that animals have told her that it makes them feel as though they were riding in a hot air balloon and someone has thrown out a big, heavy anchor so they just can't move forward in that vehicle. They feel stuck."

Is my deceased pet sad or jealous over my new pet?

When we experience love, joy, and happiness, our pets on the other side benefit from it immediately even if we're experiencing it because of a new pet that has now come into our life, or if a family member or another animal is making us happy. As long as we are experiencing an emotion of joy, they get to feel that emotion too.

It's certainly natural to grieve a departed pet; this is part of the healing process. We have to experience grief before we can get through the healing process to the other side of it. But the fact is that If you're showing love to another animal who is now down here on earth, your deceased animal will greatly benefit from this fact. They will not feel the jealousy that they would if they were still alive and you had acquired a new pet, instead they will rejoice with you.

Does my pet know how much I love him or her?

This is one of the questions most frequently asked of animal communicators and the answer is undoubtedly "Yes. They do, and far more clearly than you have any idea of."

As we have explained, animals feel your feelings as though they were theirs, they actually experience them, so when you tell them you love them they can feel your love. If for example, you say to them as you leave for work in the morning "Goodbye Toggins, I love you!" They understand the words when we tell them we love them. In fact, animals understand our words and phrases much more often than we think they do even though they will respond to an image even more easily than language.

A leading animal communicator, Danielle Mackinnon, tells an interesting story of a miscommunication between herself and a horse that she was riding during her vacation that illustrates the way that animals respond to what we are "imaging" in our minds and cannot be fooled. This particular horse had been described to her as a difficult one and before their ride, she was trying to convince the horse that she was friendly so that there would be no need for him to be oppositional.

However, because she had told been told that he was oppositional in nature, at the same time that she was saying encouraging things to this horse she was secretly visualizing obstructive behavior on his part and in fact she got exactly that behavior from him! When she realized that she must change her mental imagery and see in her mind's eye the horse behaving in a cooperative fashion, only then did things change and he began to act that way.

In other words, if we fear a certain behavior on the part of an animal and are visualizing the negative, we will be likely to get it. However, if we send them the images that are encouraging and supportive the animal will correspondingly react to positive visualization that we have in our minds rather to than any words.

Do our pets come into our lives to help us?

Many animal communicators refer to the fact that in their conversations with pets the latter show deep concern for the feelings of their loved humans and will attempt to help make them feel better the minute they perceive their human is in distress. In fact, animals have many times been known to make people they love who are ill or upset, depressed or lonely frightened or otherwise troubled, feel much better. Often they succeed in doing this.

According to animal communicators, pets will repeatedly express concern about their humans and often we can trace strange and puzzling behaviors on the part of an animal to the fact that they are mirroring the upsets of their owners. If we are secretly bothered by something we are not directly facing, the animal may inadvertently call this to our attention by expressing disruptive behavior which gets our attention.

I remember a time when I tripped and fell and suffered a severe strain of my back and my cat Dandy, who was the other side of a closed hallway door, realized that I had been injured and began yowling at the top of his lungs in an attempt to reach me. His desperate wish to help was unmistakable and even though I didn't understand animal communication in any formal sense at that time – I had not studied it and was not born with this ability as some people are – I could clearly hear the distress in my cat's voice, he was almost breaking down the door to get to me.

We will talk about the way in which our pets serve as our teachers and guides in many instances, in the final chapter of this book when we take a look at the gifts that our animals bring to us.

Do our animals come into our life for a reason?

I personally believe that very little that happens to us is just "happenstance" and that far more of it occurs for some reason that we usually have no idea of. I cannot prove that and it really doesn't make any difference whether any of us believe it in terms of our becoming much more sensitive to the feelings of animals.

If our pets are sent to us specifically to help us in our often confusing paths through this life, then this is a beautiful way to look at them and one that can benefit us regardless of whether we can prove this theory. While the lessons they bring might not always be what we want, they may be exactly what we need in a given instance. But isn't this true of any true lessons that life has to offer us?. Many of the most profound learning experiences in our lives have not been very pleasant at the time but may have been exactly what we could benefit from the most.

How do animals feel about euthanasia?

Animal communicators report that the animals they work with seem to look upon it as just one more way of transitioning, and do not experience it as an "attack" on them. As we have pointed out, animals are quite comfortable with the idea that it is their "time to go" when they feel it is, and at this point they may even experience anticipation at the start of a new phase of existence.

Communicators do comment that animals occasionally show an instinctive resistance at the last minute to euthanasia, such as reflex movements, growls, or other signs of momentary distress and this can sometimes upset pet owners and cause them to feel guilty. Karen believes the animals do not retain that moment as a part of their conscious memory as they never seem to recall these happenings when they speak from the afterlife. Furthermore, she feels that any signs of struggle are natural born reflexes as the animal's body is programmed with a strong will to survive. Many times a sedative is given by a veterinarian to help calm a distressed animal prior to euthanasia. This can result in slowing down the circulation, causing the animal to appear to fight or struggle for its last breath.

Animal communicator Danielle Mackinnon feels that such reflexive reactions actually represent an instinctiver last minute "burst of life", giving the animal the force necessary to pass away to the other side. This concept would make them act the way a rocket fires off–the sizzling and spluttering gives the rocket the energy to blast off.

Whatever the exact experience at the time of passing, it is seemingly not remembered or even considered after the animal transitions.

Are animals who have physical defects, either inborn or acquired, distressed by this fact?

One of the lessons animals teach us stems from their natural acceptance of the way they themselves are. You will see this in Chapter 12 where I write about the cat Timmy who had a crippling disease from which he eventually died but Timmy was a totally happy cat during his lifetime, it was his owner who was distressed by his handicaps, not him.

Along these same lines, here is a quote by animal communicator Danielle Mackinnon of an incident which illustrates the total acceptance of their own condition, whatever it may be, by animals. She shared this telling account with her own email list and I reprint it here with her kind permission. It concerns a dog she connected to at the request of a student in one of her animal communication classes. This is what Danielle writes:

"As I connected to this dog, I immediately heard something like, "I'm awesome! And everything I do is wonderful! And I have no behavior problems. And I'm totally happy!"

And as I heard this, I thought to myself - "He who doth protest too much..." I wasn't quite believing this spunky dog. Is he that happy and well-behaved and awesome ALL the time?

So, I told my student what her dog was saying to me and that I thought it was unlikely that he was that perfectly behaved and happy every minute of the day?

I asked her if this was making sense to her and she kind of scrunched her face up in a way that indicated she wasn't quite "buying" it either.

So, I told her I wanted to find out what was really going on and to do that I was going to go to the "soul level". (The soul level is where animals talk about the big picture, the lessons they are teaching their humans and more. It's also the place where there really isn't ego and total truth always comes through.)

As I went to the soul level with this dog, I was bombarded with... yes - the same information! He was still talking to me about how happy he was and how great he felt and how much he was enjoying his life.

I had to share this with my student.

"So, here's the thing. He's not changing his tune. He really is saying that he's happy and content and well-behaved and just awesome all the time. And now, I do believe him!"

My student scrunched up her face again, "That's what he keeps telling everyone I know who can communicate with animals! But he has deformed paws and he trips and falls sometimes and he's getting older and he sometimes poops on the floor..." and she listed all of the things that he was doing that were upsetting her. Her heart was breaking for him.

And here's what was so exciting about this reading: her dog knew that she was upset and worried that he wasn't OK and he had a plan to nip those worries right in the bud.

He didn't waste time answering my questions or telling me about his life, Danielle writes, -

instead, he went straight to the heart of the matter.

He told us how great he is. How happy he is. How well-behaved he is. And he meant it. And he meant for her to finally get that and stop worrying and see things from his point of view - not hers.

And I believe, that is what she took away from the reading. Even though it may look one way to her, this dog is still having a grand old time. Only SHE cares if he trips. He just gets up and keeps on going, laughing at himself all the way."

That is quite a lesson for all of us, isn't it?

CHAPTER TWELVE

Connecting With A Pet In The Afterlife

For some people, this chapter may seem a bit difficult because it speaks of visits from the afterlife, which of course presupposes that there is an afterlife. This personal belief is not adopted by everyone, nor is it necessary in order to derive a deep understanding of your pet at the time of his or her passing, and to experience much comfort from the accounts given here.

I suggest that you allow your heart to dictate your response when you read the poignant experiences of the apparent "separations "of animals from their beloved owners. You may be amazed at the insight you will gain into your pet's experience of passing, whether that be in the past or at some future time,

There is no doubt that we are dealing here with one of the most painful experiences that people ever face. As a professional who has counseled many human beings who have lost those close to them, both human and animal, I have noticed that the loss of a beloved animal can be as intensely difficult as the death of another beloved human being. It can sometimes be even more devastating in a particular instance than the death of a person in one's human family. We will take a look at why this may be so when we consider the gifts that pets bring us in the final chapter of this book.

The Passing of Skylar

I reprint below a tribute written by a dog owner who happens to be a leading online marketer who sent this piece out to his list, and I just accidentally happened to read it that day. His name is James Jones and he sent out the following announcement to his subscriber list of many thousands of people the day his beloved dog, Skylar, died. I am bringing to you, word for word, what I think echoes the experiences of almost everyone who has ever lost a pet whom they treasure.

I don't know James Jones personally, but since his article on Skylar resonated with me so powerfully I asked his permission to reprint it in this book, and he has graciously granted me that permission. Here is what he wrote about Skylar on the day she died. It was directed to his newsletter subscribers consisting of many thousands of people.

Note from James Jones

"To All of You"

"I debated with myself on whether to send you this email or not. I don't discuss my personal life much online because I like to keep my private life private. And I certainly don't want to start your week off with bad news.

But I haven't emailed you in several days and you may have noticed and wondered what was up because I tend to email every day rain or shine

There is one member of my family you may have heard me talk about though. I've mentioned her in my emails and on my podcast. At the start of just about every webinar I'm on, someone enters the chat and asks, "How's Skylar?"

On many of my instructional videos, you will hear the distinct "Jingle, Jingle, Jingle" of Skylar's collar as she gets up and shakes (which actually means, *"Hey, won't you stop playing with that machine and pay attention to me for a minute!"*)

Skylar was with me for 14 years. Before I even started working online full time there was Skylar.

When I was working my corporate job during the day, doing online marketing on weekends and living in a small cramped condo with no backyard, here was Skylar.

When I was still writing code myself until the wee hours of the morning, there was Skylar.

Even at 14 she was still a very active dog and it was just in the last 6 months that she stopped chasing and catching the Frisbie -- and that's only because we made the decision that it was probably not a good idea for an old lady to be jumping up and landing on her fragile hips and legs.

So she switched to chasing a ball which we would kick across the yard. No big deal. She always won the game. She always got the ball before anyone else.

Last week she stopped chasing the ball.

That was probably the hardest part for me. Because she had stopped doing the thing she loved to do -- the thing she lived to do.

This weekend she stopped eating. She even turned her nose up at her favorite thing in the world: a fried egg.

The past two days she was panting heavily and obviously having problems breathing.

At noon today she was barely moving. I called her vet (who has treated her since she was 6 weeks old) and he came to our house to help her go gently.

And she did. Her final gift to me. At 2:30 PM ET Skylar passed peacefully, surrounded by friends.

She was 14 years, 5 months and 25 days old. Old for a dog. Ancient for a Boxer.

She had a great life. And she enriched the lives of many. There was not a human being she did not immediately love. Especially kids. She had a certain instinct about children. She knew when to play rough and when to be as gentle as a feather.

My mother used to own a daycare center. She would have about 12 or 14 kids at a time in the play room watching TV. Skylar would go from one to the next to the next giving them kisses. Then she would start at the first child again and go around over and over again.

One little girl was afraid of dogs, so she would put a blanket over her head. When Skylar got to her she would pause for a couple of seconds and wait to see if she would put down the blanket. Then Skylar would keep with her rotation.

After about the 4th time the little girl finally gave in and took the blanket off her head. Skylar licked her face like it was a lollipop. The little girl giggled with glee and kept yelling for Skylar to "give me another turn."

Ok, I could go on and on with the Skylar stories. (maybe I'll write a book) but I'll close out now.

Skylar I'm going to miss you girl. You were truly one of a kind.

James

Comment By Pat

I don't know about you but I start to tear up every time I read that Skyler story. I think James Jones has expressed the feelings in the heart of every pet owner who loses that brilliant center of their life which they call, for want of a better word, "my pet".

Now I am going to bring you some of the stories that Karen has to tell about departed pets who have sent messages through her, as an animal communicator, to their loved owners. I think these will help you deal with your own loss more easily and perhaps bring understanding about certain things that may have puzzled you in the past.

In Part Two of this book, the section where I give helpful tools for all pet owners who want to get closer with their pets, I give you some Choices Affirmations to use for when your pet dies. Hopefully, these will be helpful in mitigating the pain you may feel and bring back to you the joy of having this animal friend near you who inhabited your life so fully on earth for however long they remained here.

I want you to hear Karen's experiences as told in her own words to get the full impact of them, so below I have reprinted an entire chapter from her book *Hear All Creatures* in which Karen addresses this subject. Whether or not you entirely believe what she says is less important by far than whether you are open to the understanding it will bring you for your own pet's passing if you allow it to do so.

She commences by telling us about a much loved departed cat named Tabby, whose owner not only felt devastated at the loss of her close companion but also guilty because she feared she had not done enough to mitigate her cat's illness.

Tabby

Karen Anderson writes about her:

"As soon as I contacted Tabby, her energy came through immediately and she asked me to tell her mom that "I'm right here by her side. I have never left."

Then the cat, quite surprisingly, went on to say "My mom mourns for me and grieves for me for no reason. There is no sadness in what happened. It was the will of the universe, and it was my time. I had other things to do and to accomplish, and she must realize this. Tell her this for me, will you?"

"I will tell her, Tabby. What other messages can you share?" I asked.

"Tell her I'm fine and that this is a beautiful place. No one can imagine the beauty it brings. We are here for now, but in time we will move on and continue our journey... Our journey continues."

"Tabby, that sounds wonderful," I said. "Tell me, what was your purpose for being with your mom, Lisa, down on earth?"

"I filled her heart with joy and I gave her the confidence she needed. She is still fighting for the confidence, and I feel her struggle. Tell her she has it in her, that she just needs to look. Perhaps hearing from me will encourage her to find her inner strength. Perhaps now she will start on her way on the path to finding that strength."

"Perhaps she will, Tabby. I will tell her, But did you know that your mom still agonizes over your death and that she blames herself for it? How do you feel about that?"

"There is no reason to blame herself. This is the work of higher energies that determine what will be. She needs to realize that love never ends. It conquers all, and with this love in her heart, she can conquer all. She is being tested right now, and part of her test came from me leaving. But now she is still learning about her limits and her strengths, and she needs to know she has power beyond what she thinks. She just needs to pay attention to it."

"Then you don't hold her responsible for your passing?"

"No, my child, there is no one man or woman on this earth who can be responsible for what the elders decide. There are great energies at work beyond our consciousness. We do not determine things like life or death. She needs to know that she is not responsible for my time on earth. My time on earth is written as the will and will be what it is. No one can alter that.

Then Tabby continued, "So Please tell her to release these feelings of blame and guilt and to rejoice in the lessons of love that she has learned. She opened her heart to me as she has not opened her heart to others. That was what needed to happen and it did. It happened. Great things will come to her. Tell her to focus and pay attention and great things will come."

"I will tell her, Tabby. What other message do you have for Lisa? "

"Tell her I am wise beyond what she realizes. And I have been in spirit now and will continue to learn far faster than on earth. Our time here in spirit is no comparison to your time there. You cannot comprehend our time."

"Do you feel good?" I asked.

"I feel fine, I feel good! I have no pain, no worry, no regrets, I am complete. My energy completes itself here. We see all being rejuvenated while we are here. It is our filling stop. We stop here and rest, and we're filled up with the knowledge to continue our journey."

"So you are not alone?"

"No, not at all. There are many of us here, all at our own pace. There is not a time frame. We do not have to come or go at any certain time, just when we're ready and feel fulfilled. Then we continue on."

"Then what happens?"

"We go to our next place,".

"You mean back to this earth?"

"Yes, if that is the will."

"The will of the universe?"

"Yes, if that is the will. Then we come back, and we continue to learn and to grow. We all grow on earth and learn lessons, then we come here to be refreshed. It is nice here."

"Please tell me more about it."

"It is glorious, it is magnificent, it is all encompassing, and it is LOVE.

"So you feel loved?"

"We all feel loved. This is our Creator and we are all loved."

"So will your journey take you back to Lisa?"

"Perhaps. I feel she has more to learn."

"And you think you can teach her?"

"I already taught her much. Her lessons were valuable and she completed them well."

"What did you teach her?"

"Compassion and trust."

"These are wonderful lessons and I'm sure she appreciates that."

"Yes, but she wastes it on blame. Tell her not to waste it. It is not necessary to waste such lessons on things like blame and guilt. These are not valued traits. They are worthless and take away from our value. Tell her to pay attention to the good, what she learned in her heart, and to know that I am with her every day. I feel her pain and can do nothing but wait."

"Wait for what?"

"For her to realize that I am fine and she is fine too. Once she realizes this, it will   all be..."

"Will all be what?

"Complete..."

"Oh, I see. So you'd like your mom, Lisa, to focus on the good, the lessons in the things she learned from you..."

"Yes. I opened her heart to these difficult things, and now she must continue her path."

"I see. Well, thank you, Tabby. You have really helped me and your mom to understand things a little better. I hope you realize how much she loves you."

"Oh, I do. Hers is love like no other."

"She continues to send her love to you."

"And I to her.".

"Go in peace, my friend, Tabby, until we meet again."

"You as well. Goodbye."

Lisa's reply did not come to me that day, but later, through the following email. She wrote:

Dear Karen,

Since hearing Tabby's thoughts and wisdom, I have filled a spot in my heart with joy that was sad for so long. I feel that this experience helped me realize the joy in my life and that blame and guilt are qualities that should not be stressed about for a long period. Tabby said she lifted my heart with joy and gave me the confidence I needed. By releasing blame and guilt in my life, my confidence has grown more than I could ever guess. Tabby's words are helping me beyond what I ever imagined is possible. I hope that I am making her proud and passing the tests that I believe she gives me... Thank you again, Karen, for this experience. - Lisa

Comment By Pat:

When reading this chapter I suggest that you allow yourself to just "flow with" the words of these stories of the afterlife and not try to figure out how an animal can be so wise and all-knowing as Tabby is depicted in this account. There is much we do not know about the true souls of animals, who they really are, and why they have come to us. I did not know how my cat Dandy could be so wise as to help me write a book after he died, as he told Karen he wanted to do when we had our consultation, but look at what has happened – this book has been an eye-opening experience for me from beginning to end and – call it my imagination if you will – it really doesn't make any difference since everything worthwhile in the history of human evolution always appears first in our imaginations anyway – but I "know" in some way that I feel Dandy's presence and wisdom in the book as it is unfolding. It is only up to me to convey this and it almost seems as though he were some sort of Master Author. We do not need to know "the absolute truth" of everything about life-and-death because we can still feel instinctively the love and devotion and meaning for us of our dearest pets. So, I suggest you just flow with these stories and let them speak to you in whatever way they want.

Baron (as described in Karen's words)

Baron was a German Shepherd dog who passed away at seven years of age from a heart condition. At the time when his owner Dave heard that I was an animal communicator Baron was still living and so Dave asked for a consultation for him. He had a very close bond with this dog whose health had recently taken a sharp turn for the worse. Dave was concerned that Baron was barely eating and was "just not himself.".

Without letting Dave give me any more facts about Baron, I contacted this dog telepathically and he told me enthusiastically about the close connection he had with Dave, his human dad, and how fun his life was in the mountains, running through the woods and playing in the streams with Dave and his other dog, Reka. Baron showed me his favorite place in their house; a big sunlit room filled with floor-to-ceiling windows, and plants.

When I asked Baron how he felt now, his energy shifted, however. He told me he didn't feel that well and that his "heart hurt". I asked him if the pain in his heart was emotional or physical. Baron replied that it was an actual pain. He had no idea why his appetite was failing, but told me that he felt it was his "time to go." Baron said to send his love to his dad and asked me to tell him how very special Dave makes him feel.

I gave the messages to Dave, and quite naturally, he was deeply upset. When I mentioned that Barron's heart hurt, Dave was amazed, because only he and his vet knew that Barron suffered from a heart condition. He had not shared this information with anyone else.

As Dave listened to more messages from Baron, he grew very quiet. This man couldn't imagine life without Baron. They were constant companions and best friends.

Upon questioning, Dave confirmed that his mountain home had a large entryway, with floor-to-ceiling windows that were full of his wife's plants. It was as Baron described although I had never been to their home to see it. Dave said that Barron loved to lie in that room so he could see everything that was going on outside. He also told me how he would take Baron and Reka, his other dog, on long walks through the Rocky Mountains, and the dogs would splash and play in the stream near the house.

Following our session, the vet continued to run tests on Baron over the next few days to find out what was happening with his failing health.

And then about a week later I was notified that Barron had passed into the spirit world. Dave had buried him on a hill overlooking the banks of the stream where he and Reka played. Dave thanked me for the messages from Baron and said they brought him great comfort.

Two weeks later, however, I was quietly meditating at home when Baron's energy unexpectedly appeared to me. Baron told me he had an urgent message for Dave and that he needed to talk to me right away. When I agreed to talk he told me that he was very concerned that Dave was still agonizing over his death. He knew that his dad was full of sorrow, sadness, and loss.

Baron said this made him very upset, and requested that I contact Dave right away to tell him that Baron was still there, by his side. The dog said to say he would," never leave him." and that if Dave listened closely, he would hear Baron's collar jingling.

Baron said, "it was my time to go and nothing could have changed that." He wanted his dad to stop feeling guilty about his death. Instead, Baron asked that Dave remembers him as he was during all the wonderful times they had had, the great life they had shared, and the bonds of friendship that would never end.

Baron spoke with an urgency I couldn't ignore, so I made a very hesitant phone call to Dave. I hadn't spoken with him since Baron's passing, and I wasn't sure how he would take this unexpected call. Dave answered, and I told him to just listen, not to say one word. I delivered the urgent messages from Baron, then quietly hung up the phone before Dave could reply.

Several days later, Dave called me back. He told me that it was true; he had been agonizing over Baron's loss, full of sadness and dwelling on guilt over Baron's death. He was blaming himself for not being able to find out what was wrong with Baron before he died, and so have been able to postpone his death. Dave said that at first, he was a little stunned by Baron's messages from the spirit world. But once he thought about it, he realized that his dog was still with him.

Dave then shifted his thoughts to all the wonderful times he and Baron had experienced together and the closeness they had shared. He said he had even felt Baron's presence several times, and he would listen for the sound of his collar jingling.

Dave said that only Baron would have such a direct connection to his heart to know all those things about him and how badly he was struggling with the loss. Now Dave knows that the bonds of love are everlasting. They do not end with death.

It has been several years now since Baron passed into the spirit world. Dave still misses him in their daily walks, but now he and Reka take Kit, his new "rescued" German Shepherd, through the mountains to play in the streams. And Dave knows in his heart that Barron is right there by his side.

Karen continues by telling about Calia

Calia's "mom", Janet, called me soon after her little dog had passed. This seven-year-old schnauzer had died suddenly, leaving Janet devastated.

Her grieving owner was initially skeptical of my animal communication process and only came to me because her best friend had strongly urged her to come. She asked me if there would be any specific messages from Calia so she could tell if it was really her beloved dog that was coming through.

I assured her that I would be able to connect with Calia's energy, bringing many aspects of her personality and behavior to the session. I also reminded her that I have no control over what animals tell me. I can ask questions, but only they control their answers.

Our tearful phone session started on a sunny morning. I was in my office in Elk, Washington, and Janet was in Colorado. As our session began, immediately Calia sent Janet many loving messages and told her how sorry she was to see her mom in so much pain. Calia reassured her mom that she was okay and adjusting to her new life in the spirit world. There were many heartfelt messages that came through, bringing much-needed relief and tears of joy. As we neared the end of the session, Janet asked Calia what her favorite memory was of their life together.

Calia said to me, "Tell her "water in the grass...water in the grass."

Okay, I thought to myself, I've learned to just say whatever messages come through, no matter how strange they may sound to me.

"I'm supposed to tell you that her favorite memory is "water in the grass," I said.

There was silence on the other end of the phone, and then a sharp intake of breath. "Oh, my dear!" Janet said, then softly started to cry.

"Tell me, Janet, what does this mean? What is water in the grass?"

Janet told me through her tears that her backyard had several levels. On one level she had a park bench next to a water fountain. One of her favorite things to do with her cat had been to go out back, sit on this bench and, as the water splashed out of the fountain onto the lawn, Calia would bite at the water in the grass. It was a simple pleasure that they both enjoyed, and Calia knew that it was the message her mom needed to hear right now.

That message that Calia sent left Janet speechless. Even from the spirit world, Calia relayed specific memories of their life together in such a simple way. Water in the grass... Sometimes it's the little things in life that mean the most.

Karen tells us about "Seeing Spots"

Denise and her mother, Margaret, came to the Spokane Expo in June 2006 to check in on several of their animal companions, both living and deceased, and Denise asked if I would first connect with Sophie, who had recently passed.

Both Denise and Margaret were listening intently to Sophie's messages as I connected with this pretty gray and white kitten. Denise explained that she wanted to make sure that Sophie had made it to the other side so that the cat could come back to her again in this or another lifetime.

Denise told me that she had agonized over the decision to euthanize Sophie some five weeks earlier at about the same time that her mother's dog, Blanche, had passed. Denise still held much guilt and grief over Sophie's passing. What she didn't realize was that her emotional ties to Sophie were keeping the cat earthbound and unable to continue her journey to the Light.

As I connected with Sophie, I saw telepathically that her claws were firmly gripping the earth. She was not wanting to let go. She clearly needed my help. Confused and not sure of what to do myself, I showed Sophie how there were angels right there to help her cross over to the other side so she could continue her journey.

With some simple visualizations from me. It, Sophie slowly started to release her grip on the earth.

Denise then admitted that she was to blame for holding on to Sophie emotionally. She now realized that she was being selfish by doing this and it was not helping Sophie's journey. As I began to encourage Sophie to move toward her angels, at that point Sophie sent me a clear message that she was "seeing spots."

"Why would she tell me that she is seeing spots?" I asked Denise, not sure what this message meant.

"I don't know," Denise shrugged, trying herself to understand what the "spots" could be.

Sophie was still reluctant to leave the earth plane, so I had to call upon her angels again and this time ask them to act as if they were a cavalry and to make this transition dramatic and compelling. They responded as though they were indeed a cavalry with horns blaring, coming over a rise. It was quite a fabulous divine scene. The angels came and surrounded Sophie with love and let her know all was safe.

However, despite all of this, Sophie still felt she couldn't let go.

"She still doesn't want to let go," I told Denise and her mother.

Her mother Margaret then asked me if Sophie could see her dog Blanche, Sophie's close companion when they were on earth? If she could, she said, that would mean that Sophie could now make it to the spirit world. I asked Margaret to describe Blanche to me so I could picture her in my mind, and Margaret immediately emailed me Blanche's picture.

When I looked at the picture, I couldn't believe what I saw. Blanche was a border collie mix with huge black-and-white spots all over her!

Sophie was very clearly saying, "spots", and by so doing was actually saying, "Blanche!" And by doing this, Sophie was letting me know she was now able to let go and make it to the other side because Blanche would be at her side.

"She's seeing spots!" I said, "Blanche is spotted! She has big cow spots all over her!"

Denise and Margaret now "got it". They realized that the spot reference was to Blanche! Sophie was so happy we all finally got the message that she started to make me laugh and smile.

It was a funny way of putting it all together, but we all finally got it!

Timmy

When I first saw a photo of Timmy, he stole my heart. He had that effect on people. This beautiful little black and white kitten had the face of an angel and a heart of gold.

He had suffered all his life from numerous afflictions, including Spina Bifida, or a curvature of the spine, and cerebellar hyperplasia, which causes jerky movements or tremors.

Spina Bifida. The vertebrae fail to close normally around the spinal cord, leading to motor and sensory problems in areas that are affected by nerves. The Manx deformity can cause cats to suffer from this problem because it is associated with the gene for taillessness. Symptoms can also include a hopping gait and incontinence.

Timmy's "mom", Jamie, is a special needs expert who had intentionally adopted Timmy because of his affliction and her own conviction that she could help him, which she was certainly able to do through her love.

Although Timmy had many physical challenges, the love poured from him, and he had many friends. He would lie on his towel with his "Kitty friends", or play with toys and even watch movies on the big screen. Timmy especially liked the "movie with dogs," he told me one day. Jamie laughed as she remembered that another cat must have stepped on the remote and changed the channel to a dog show. Timmy loved to watch dogs on the big screen.

Jamie also took Timmy to his regular cerebral sacral therapy sessions to help stimulate nerves and improve his overall health. When I checked in with Timmy, he said he loved his therapy sessions and he especially loved to go places with his mom.

Timmy fit nicely into a special sling that Jamie made for him, and he traveled with her as she ran errands or spent time outside in the sunshine. He was truly the joy of her life. He never complained, even with all the physical challenges he faced. He shared only his love and devotion to his mom and his favorite toys.

On a late winter evening, I got a call from Jamie. Timmy had passed away suddenly, unexpectedly, and she was devastated. There had been little that Jamie or anyone else could do. Rushed to the emergency vet clinic, Timmy's one-year-old body failed him, and he slipped away in Jamie's arms. It was only a few days later that Jamie asked if I would connect with Timmy for her. She was feeling guilty and blamed herself for his sudden demise. "I should have taken him in sooner." she agonized.

Jamie's pain was obvious as I drew Timmy's energy to me. He sent his love to her right away. "From the heart of my soul." He said as he came through vibrant and glowing. He showed me a brilliant light that was shining on him, and said that it felt "really good, better than the sunshine."

Timmy showed me that he was surrounded with joy and laughter and that he was in a place of celebration. Timmy then went on to describe his purpose in life with Jamie, and how his suffering on earth had earned him a special kind of privilege. "Joyous movement occurred when I transitioned." He explained. "A celebration of life, not of death. It moved me closer to the eternal one, the one being of Light, our Creator, the divine."

Then Timmy described how his soul evolved to the highest level, that of the divine masters.

"I am of that realm now," he stated, "all the events of my life are now understood, all meaningful. Now I can give back wisdom, knowledge, soul growth, peace and, tranquility... Everything a person yearns for. Tell mom not to be sad. Her life will be richer because of this. I see it on the higher plane from a higher viewpoint. We couldn't have progressed anymore, we limited out. I will bring others in who need you, mom."

In closing, Timmy told Jamie to stay connected with him through prayer and meditation, then he pulled his energy away.

It was hardly a day later when Serengeti entered Jamie's life. Serengeti was born with Manx syndrome. The gene causes spinal defects and can be fatal, but Serengeti is dealing well with her disability.

According to Denise, Serengeti is a happy little girl, and full of energy. She doesn't know that she has a disability. She gets around well and likes to play with her new friends. She loves people and especially loves her new mom, Jamie.

Karen's Visualization and Prayer for Release

If animals are still emotionally attached to us at the time of their passing and do not want to leave their body, it is possible, as in the case of Sophie, that they will hold on tightly to the earth plane and be unable to continue their journey. On the other hand, some animals will refuse to go because they don't want to upset us or cause us pain. Karen points out that it's always best to give our animal companions permission to continue their journey into the spirit world, so they may continue their greater spiritual journey back home to the place of infinite love.

To help an animal who is reluctant to pass away, Karen suggests that you visualize your animal being surrounded by beautiful angels, and imagine the Angels spreading their wings wide surround your animal with loving warmth and wrap them in their beauty as you say the following prayer and continue to imagine the glow as the Angels comfort and calm your animal. A simple prayer will help animals release their ties to the earth and set them free to continue their journey. Any prayer you feel comfortable with that has real meaning to you may be used.

This one is Karen's favorite:

I call upon the Angels of love and mercy, and ask them to surround (insert the name of the animal) who has passed into spirit: I ask that you allow (insert name of animal) to release the bonds that hold (him or her), and give (him or her) wings to fly into the heavens. Surround (him or her) with your love and warmth, and comfort (him or her) on their journey. I give (insert animal's name) permission to continue on the path to glory, and the Divine. Amen.

A Time to Die

Karen is by no means the only animal communicator who is repeatedly told by many different animals whom they contact from the afterlife that the animal feels perfectly comfortable with the fact that there has been a "right time for them to die". It is usually the owner who is upset and all too often guilty because they did not prevent what they could not prevent, the animal, however, is perfectly comfortable with the situation ...and typically has no regrets about it.

Animal communicator, Danielle Mackinnon, reports this instance of "a time to die" reported by an animal during their session with her. She writes:

"Recently I worked with a woman named Kate who was concerned about her cat, Dodo. When we got this client and her cat on the phone I asked Kate if it would fit what she was observing if I told her that her cat was feeling that she could barely drag her body around and was spacey and depressed, and she said that was exactly what she was seeing. As we progressed through the reading, Kate was crying at times. Interestingly, though, I never felt tears and that was because Kate asked me the question she had been dreading for weeks.

"Danielle, I need to know if it's time for him to cross over," she said as she cried quietly into the phone. While she was asking this question, in the back of my head I heard Dodo talking over her. He was saying, "I'm ready whenever you are."

When I passed this message on to her Kate she started weeping even harder. She then told me that her family, friends, and vet had all been telling her that it was his time to go, but she had resisted this information. I was happy to be able to help her understand what Dodo was saying about his desire to cross over while at the same time he had great love for her and she was helped to make her decision about his euthanasia.

Danielle MacKinnon goes on to say that every day she runs into situations, whether through her Facebook page, a private session, an email or something else that lets her know that an animal has reached his or her time to leave this earth plane and that she finds that the animal is quite content with this knowledge, differently than most humans would be. She is so grateful for each and every time she gets the opportunity to help even one person understand how simple it is for their animal when they are "ready to pass away."

And now we will go to the final chapter of Part One of this book where we will look at the gifts that our treasured pets bring to us. It is a profound subject that has no boundaries but is experienced worldwide and probably has been throughout all eras of human history.

CHAPTER THIRTEEN

Amazing Gifts Our Pets Give Us

To describe all the gifts our animals give to us would be an impossible task, but this chapter will give you at least a partial list. You will add to it in your mind by thinking of your own pet.

Pets Can Be Wonderful Role Models

Of central importance to us are the life lessons our pets teach us wordlessly, through their example. They can be superb role models for us and the more conscious of this fact that we are the more value we can derive from it.

Here is a list of just some of the valuable qualities our pets can embody for us:

1. Love without judgment or conditions, an innocent total love that comes primarily from the heart, not the brain. For Karen, this is probably a fascinating part of her calling. She believes our animal friends are here to be the best examples they can possibly be for us, to be in the moment, to not judge, and to accept us the way we are. They are here for us and they don't care if we're a criminal or a nun. They don't care if we're employed or not. They don't care. It simply doesn't matter to them.

2. Unquestioned forgiveness no matter what the other person or animal does.

3. Complete authenticity, no deceptions are possible for an animal and they will teach you how you can be more authentic if you let them.

4. Total joy in living whenever they get a chance to experience this, often many times a day, over and over again.

5. Being able to live in the present. Our pets love and thrive on being in the moment. They teach us that "right now" is what it is all about. Right now, here in this moment, loving life, enjoying this sunspot or curling up in their favorite "place" to sleep, enjoying running through a field or chewing on a bone - whatever it is they are doing is what they thrive on. They are enjoying the moment. All the other "nonsense" that humans conjure up outside of being in the moment is ridiculous to them.

6. The impulse to help others no matter what it takes to do this – to instantly "be there" for them. Remember how the seeing-eye cat, Ginger, helped her best friend Jack navigate when he had become blind?

7. No worrying about "the future" or the "past" – our pets illustrate for us repeatedly how to live in the present in the most vivid fashion.

8. Being totally non-judgmental. Judgement of others or oneself is simply not possible for an animal,

it is not in their "vocabulary". They show this to us repeatedly each day

Tangible Gifts

In addition to the wonderful traits they model for us, our pets give us tangible gifts that are of inestimable value. Here are a few:

1. They let us know that another living being - our pet - is sensitively aware of us and that they want to be with us for no reason other than that we are us. This fact reminds us repeatedly throughout every day that we are important because we are "ourselves" and that we do not have to be any more than that.

2. Our animal friends afford us amazing relief from the pressures that we face when we constantly interact with other human beings. People have confusing institutions and conventions which cause us much stress, usually this occurs during most of the day. Our pets bring us a much-needed vacation from the complexities of human life that we may not realize is putting such a strain on us.

3. Our pets afford us "no strings attached" enjoyment from playing with them, talking to them, walking with them, watching their antics, cuddling up with them, or just plain being with them.

Special Lessons And/Or Protections From Our Pets

1. The lesson of unwavering love.

2. The lesson of what it means to experience complete forgiveness for anything we might do or have done, big or little, that might have displeased our animal.

3. Physical Protection through a pet's unending vigilance.

4. Loyalty that is unshakeable –it is always there and is ever renewed.

5. AND FINALLY, OUR PETS OPEN OUR OWN HEARTS, fully and completely and with no reservation. This may, in fact, be their greatest gift to us, the most important lesson that animals have to give to us. In essence, they teach us how to LOVE.

How to Appreciate Your Own Pet in a New Way

As a way of expressing your appreciation for your pet, I suggest you make a list of their unique gifts to you.

You can do this by taking a pad of paper (or opening a computer document) and at the top of the page write your pet's name and the date. Then, referring to the first part of this last chapter of Part 1, write down all of the ways you can think of that your special animal friend may have offered each one of these gifts I have listed (and skip a particular category if they haven't done so in that instance).

You may be surprised at what you have been taking for granted in terms of your animal's contributions to your life although you thought you fully recognized that, so this acknowledgment can be important for both of you.

Now, write down a list of the ways that your pet has outwardly gifted you by their behavior, numbering each one as you write down all the ways that you can think of at this moment that this animal has brought something truly valuable to you. These may be special times that you've had with them when you came together in wordless companionship or faced certain challenges together, or it may be something totally different from that. A list of good feelings that your pet has evoked in you will be of great value later if you reread it.

You may also want to put down the ways in which your pet may be serving as a role model for certain traits that you would like to develop in the future.

For example, my cat Dandy served to model for me incredible "patience". When he would go to the glass door to ask to be let out, when I opened the sliding door to let him out, he would (always to my amazement!) more often than not just stand perfectly still at the door for maybe two or three minutes, sniffing the air and gazing about before deciding whether to actually go out.

Frequently he would seat himself on the threshold of the door and just quietly contemplate the landscape. I couldn't imagine why he wanted to take all that time to make up his mind about something he had asked for, but he seemed to love doing that.

The fact is that infinite time existed for Dandy, the "eternal present", and he obviously loved his moments spent appraising the whole "going out" scene. "Do I really WANT to do this?" "Is it what I want to do NOW?", you could almost see these questions running through his mind.

Dandy taught me what it means to really take the time to consider many options and make quiet, deliberate choices about what we do. Actually we humans tend to make "plans" rather than choices, and then think we have to adhere to those plans "come hell or high water" as the old saying goes.

But Dandy could wait indefinitely until he finally had a feeling that he wanted to act in a certain way, and then, slowly, he would go out. The only exception to this was when he saw a squirrel or other animal that it would be so much fun to chase – that would catapult him into action. Otherwise...infinite patience was the name of the game– a careful consideration of what he really wanted to do right now.

I can also think of another pet of mine that acted as a role model for me.

My adorable (now departed) Welch Corgi dog, Jaffy, used to wave her ears up and down for minutes at a time, calling to passers-by on the street in delighted greeting, from our car window. She was not at all bothered when they didn't wave back. She did this to express her delight with the human race – Jaffy loved people and "had" to express that, never mind whether they gave it back!... Can you imagine a more wonderful way to be?

Jaffy Carrington

I would like you to think about what behavior your pet may be demonstrating, or that a former pet has demonstrated in the past, that might be a great idea for you to try on "for size". Something that would require you stretching yourself, "doing yourself differently" for a change.

And I suggest that you don't let the list of behaviors you come up with that you'd like to emulate ever be complete. It should be ever-expanding, always added to. It will clarify for you what is probably already in your own heart, the qualities you already value so highly in your pet, and this will help you to glean even more joy from having them in your life, or in the case of a departed pet, for having had them closely with you during the time that you did.

And now...

You are ready to proceed to Part Two of this book which consists of a series of exercises that can be a source of ready inspiration to you that can deepen your relationship with your pet and teach you how to help him or her even more effectively in times of trouble. It will also help you to handle any problems that might arise for you in relation to your animal. Part Two of this book can turn out to be an ever-present resource in times of trouble.

PART TWO

HELPFUL CHOICES
FOR PET OWNERS

CHAPTER FOURTEEN

How To Use "Choices" For A Pet

In Part One of this book we talked about your pet's inner life – in Part Two, we will now give you direct help in interacting with them more effectively.

Here are some exercises to help you build an even closer relationship with your pet. It is a collection of troubleshooting strategies for when you run into difficult phases of your relationship with your pet or when something happens to them which is upsetting to you –if they become ill, or have an accident, get lost, start engaging in puzzling behaviors or in some other way become a concern for you. Or perhaps your pet has passed away and you are experiencing this painful loss –we bring you strategies to help you through these difficult times.

This Section is an ever-present help in trouble, you can keep it handy to use whenever you need to.

In it, we give you a number of different exercises to assist you in deepening your relationship with your pet. These are based largely, but not entirely, on a special kind of stress management method known as "The Choices Method" (the word "Choices" is used in this method with a capital "C") that can help you avoid the difficulties many people encounter when using traditional affirmations.

How Does It Do This?

"Choices" work because traditional affirmations are purposely constructed to be contrary to fact – when making an affirmation you state as true a condition you would like to see which is actually contrary to fact. While certainly useful for some people, such affirmations can be unconvincing to others precisely because they seem so impossible and therefore so unconvincing.

Saying to yourself *"I live in a beautiful apartment flooded with light"* if in fact, you are living in a dingy sixth floor walkup, is so contrary to the truth, for example, that it can bring up many doubts in your mind and as a result can be ineffective in changing your attitude about the issue at hand.

But if you make a "Choice" to have your life be different, so that you say instead something like, *"I choose to live in a beautiful sunny apartment"* this can be a realistic, practical statement, and therefore fully convincing to you. All of us are free to make a Choice that is different from the way things are now and it won't feel as if you were "talking yourself into something". Rather, it makes your Choices statement believable and easy to make. A Choice, in the sense we use that word here, is therefore never contrary to fact because it is always possible to make a Choice while remaining completely truthful.

In this section, we give you a collection of carefully selected Choices to use for your pet. All you need to do is repeat each Choice aloud about 8 times (or for one round of tapping if you are using the stress management technique known as EFT) and that is your only task. This process is very simple and takes less than a minute to do. If you want, you can also write down your Choices on 3 x 5 index cards that you can carry around with you to re-read periodically during the day.

Below are Choices to use as needed, grouped into categories according to whatever issue you might want to address.

CHAPTER FIFTEEN

Helping A Pet In Distress

Whatever the problem, you can help your pet by telling them that you "know how they feel and love them" or by some simple act that demonstrates to them your love and concern for them.

When my cat Dandy was suffering from colon cancer, I often used a soft laser (see Resources section for information on this safe type of healing instrument for pets) the size of a flashlight, and waved the beam of it back and forth over his distended abdomen as though the beam were lightly caressing him. There is considerable evidence that in fact soft lasers reduce pain, inflammation, and swelling of an organ and can assist in healing (see Resources section). Doing this may have helped Dandy physically to some degree because he would almost inevitably calm down and stay close to my side as I continued to sweep the laser beam over his abdomen.

But even if the laser was not helping him physically (I couldn't be sure whether or not it was) it was "doing something" that indicated clearly to Dandy that I knew he was in pain and cared and wanted to help him. An animal, like a person, needs to know that you know how he/she is feeling and want to help.

If you perform a simple comforting act or tell your pet in words that you know they are in distress and you care, a number of times each day, you will begin to get across to your pet a crucial message, one that will mean more to them than anything else possibly could – the message is that YOU CARE!

Choices for This Purpose

Your animal may not understand human language, but they will sense your wish to help them if you use the following Choices. These can help you to bring about the healing you want for your pet. Your Choices can be immensely comforting to them even if their surface behavior continues to be agitated or withdrawn and even if seems to be having no effect on them.

Choice #1

"I choose to imagine a beautiful healing light surrounding (insert your pet's name)."

If you can visualize a healing light surrounding them, this can be deeply comforting. Since animals tend to think in images rather than words, your pet may readily respond telepathically to any images or thoughts you are sending to them. It can be of immense value to the animal and you as well if you imagine the healing light around them a number of different times during the day.

Choice #2

"I choose to do things that will make me happy even if my pet is ill – and know that my good mood will benefit us both."

Animals respond to a human being's moods with amazing sensitivity and if you are upset by your animal's illness, even if this upset understandably stems from your love for them, this can unfortunately make them even more upset rather than the opposite.

However, if they sense that you are still happy despite the fact that they are ill, this can act as a wonderful medicine for them.

If you can't imagine right now how you can possibly feel happy when your pet is in so much difficulty, or if it makes you feel guilty to feel happy if they are ill, this Choice can help you greatly too. Keep repeating it at various times throughout the day whenever something good happens to you during that day and you will begin to remember that your happiness will assist your pet in their recovery, or if needed, help them to experience a peaceful passing if that is what is in store for them.

Choice #3

"I choose to imagine that there is a powerful healing power within the food and water I give to (insert your pet's name here)."

If each time you give your pet water or food you imagine that this substance contains a wonderful healing power (and in fact it does because what you give to your pet to ingest contains your love, which is probably the most healing thing you can give to them) your animal will sense this and be more apt to eat or drink if this is what their body decides is best.

Contrast this with the message that they will pick up from you if you are worried about whether they are going to eat or drink what you put before them. In that case, any anxiety you are experiencing will immediately be transferred to your pet and make them less apt to want to touch the food you give them because the pet will now become even more anxious, picking it up from you – so your worried feelings will lead to exactly the opposite effect from that which you want to bring about.

To picture the food as containing a magic healing power may therefore be extremely effective in allowing your pet to feel differently about eating - if eating is truly the most healthy thing for them to do at the moment.

Choice #4

"I choose to recognize the wisdom of my pet's body, and respect its will for (insert your pet's name)"

This Choice will help you harmonize with your pet's needs, and if indeed, as was the case with my Dandy, their illness might be leading to their passing, then it will help you to begin to accept this with grace, or at least more ease.

Keep in mind the fact that your pet may already have enough difficulty contending with their own physical distress so they do not need the additional burden of your resistance to whatever nature is now directing them to do. All they need is your love and genuine understanding (and if possible your cheerfulness and optimism) as you intelligently apply whatever instructions have been given you medically.

CHAPTER SIXTEEN

Using Your Intuition For A Pet

Choice #1

"I choose to remember how I "knew" what... (insert name of your pet) and then describe how he or she acted in a particular instance and how you sensed it accurately). "

NOTE: If you can't think of an instance where you had a hunch about your pet that was useful, see if you can recall an instance where someone you were observing had such a hunch about what some animal was trying to convey.

Choice #2

"I choose to ask my pet, "What are you trying to tell me?"

You can at any time ask your pet to give you a sign that will help you understand what they want you to know, much as I instructed my cat Dandy how he could give me signals to tell me whether he was ready for euthanasia. Or you can ask them to send you a mental picture of what they want you to know since sending and receiving images is the way that animals communicate in the wild and it comes very naturally to them

When you post such a question, wait quietly for an answer to come into your mind, and if you don't get one you can add this further question:

"Is it (say whatever immediate thought comes into your mind, perhaps in the form of some picture image since that's the way animals prefer to communicate)?" The best way to do this may be to base it simply on a hunch

As you do this, you may be surprised by a new thought that springs to your own mind about what is troubling your pet. Communicating with animals on an intuitive level is a learned skill like any other. If you practice it, you will soon find yourself not only better able to communicate with your pet but you will find that you now enjoy a greater closeness with them.

Choice #3

"I choose to pretend that I can hear my pet talking to me out loud and imagine what he or she is saying."

As you repeat this Choice to yourself, you may find it increasingly easy to create imaginary conversations with your animal and find it quite fun. If you continue to do this, similar imaginary conversations will probably come to you more easily and then, one day, you may have a "strange" feeling that what you hear in your head as the answer, may actually be a true answer and that it is somehow coming from your pet. That will be the beginning of a deeper communication between you and your pet. If you continue using this Choice, you may discover actual evidence that what you imagined did, in fact, help to solve a problem that had been troubling you about your pet.

Choice #4

"I choose to have fun talking to my pet in my imagination and "hearing" what he/she has to say."

You can actually play games with your pet in which you pretend to have a conversation with him/her. If you do this they will probably catch on to the fact that you are doing something that specifically relates to them and likes to play the game. Try it!

CHAPTER SEVENTEEN

Becoming Closer To A Pet

Choice #1

"I choose to remember how (insert your pet's name) and I did (Insert a short description of something fun you did together)."

Choice #2

"I choose to remember how helpful it was to have (insert name of your pet) with me when (describe a distressing situation where his/her presence at the time was very helpful to you)."

Choice #3

"I choose to remember how wonderfully comforting it was to have (insert name of pet) with me when (insert an incident when you really appreciated having him/her there) happened."

Or choose the memory of any other outstanding moment that you had with your pet – there are probably many of them so you may have many possibilities.

CHAPTER EIGHTEEN

Seeing Problems From A Pet's Viewpoint

Choice #1

"I choose to imagine (insert name of your pet) in a quiet, peaceful state where he/she can hear my questions."

This is an important choice to make repeatedly; in fact, you can make it as many times as you like. Locate yourself close by your pet in as peaceful an environment as you can arrange. If you are at home, eliminate all distracting noises from the room if possible and settle down to be close to your pet even if it is agitated or withdrawn.

You will have much more control over your environment at home, of course, than if you are visiting your pet in a veterinary hospital where there may be many distracting noises and smells bombarding it. But if this is the case, it is even more important to convey to your pet a sense of peace and reassurance because of those disturbing factors.

Choice #2

(to repeat to yourself periodically while you are communicating with your pet)

" I choose to trust that he or she understands what I say."

Choice #3

(also to repeat to yourself periodically when you are with your pet)

" I choose to know that I can hear and understand what you say (addressed to your pet)."

Or, you can speak directly to your pet (no need for a conscious "Choice" here) by simply saying to them:

"Whatever you tell me is fine. (add the words "I love you" if you are feeling love for him/her at this moment, in which case you would say something like, "Whatever you tell me is fine. I love you!"

You can also say:

"I'm here to help you." These words can be immensely reassuring to your pet. Whether the pet is responding to your actual words or simply to your mood and feelings is irrelevant so long as they get the message that you are with them emotionally and that you want to help.

CHAPTER NINETEEN

Using Images To Communicate With A Pet

Choice #1

"I choose to create a simple picture or short movie clip in my mind that visually indicates what I want to say to my pet."

When you have chosen a simple picture or movie clip to concentrate upon then hold this image quietly in your mind.

Just inventing this image and letting it remain in your mind can be the first step when attempting to translate what you want to convey to your pet into the form of an image which will be intelligible to them. To do this it may be helpful to imagine that you have been handed only pencils or crayons to convey your message to your pet. How can you get across your idea through just a picture?

This may take some thought and you will need to be inventive. So consider it a game and make it fun for yourself. Even if you don't come up with the successful translation of words into a picture or a short mental video, you will get a new understanding of how your

Choice #2

"I choose to invent new ways to send my mental messages to my pet across 'inner space'."

This too can be a game-like experience. You are to invent ingenious ways, like a child would, of getting your messages across to your pet.

For example, you might picture your message (whatever way you want to imagine it looking like) flying through the air on the back of a bird, or imagine it being sent by air messenger in some other manner. Be creative, and feel the energy of dispatching this message to your pet in an inventive way.

Then imagine their behavior as they receive it and watch to see whether in real life they seem to be reacting to it in any way. If you try a number of different ways to transport the message to them you may hit on one that makes the animal perk up and show it is paying attention.

It probably goes without saying that it is best if you try this exercise at a time when neither you nor the animal is stressed. When both of you are relaxed and in a state of mind where you want to have fun, you will simply be playing a game together.

Choice #3

"I choose to feel that (insert name of your pet) is getting the message I'm trying to send."

This way of stating your Choice does not violate one of the cardinal rules of the Choices Method, which is that we should not choose the behavior of any other living being, but allow him/her Free Will. When you choose only to feel that your animal is behaving in a particular way you are leaving both of you free. You can choose your own feelings under any circumstances. So ask yourself – How would I like to feel about how this message is coming across? And then choose to feel that way.

Even if your pet doesn't understand what you're up to while you are playing around with it this way, he or she will probably sense that you're trying to play a game and that you expect them in some way to join in. If your pet gets into the spirit of the game at all, you have made real progress and the experience should be gratifying for both of you.

Choice #4

"I choose to notice any images that pop into my mind after I send the message to (insert pet's name) and consider whether they might just be his/her "answer".

pet struggles to communicate with you through using just the medium of images sent telepathically!

Of course, once you learn how to listen to what your animal is it is trying to tell you, expressed in spoken words , It will be easier for him/her to communicate with you because he/she will now be able to use not only images (their natural means of communication) but also some human language through telepathy, although it is not their natural way of communicating.

Here are some examples of how you might go about translating your message to your pet into picture form:

Let's say you wanted to know if your pet is experiencing pain in its left hind foot. You could create a mental image, perhaps a close-up shot as in a movie, of your pet's left hind foot, and then you might see yourself reaching over to it in a short mental "videotape", and see yourself gently touching that spot. By doing this, you are indicating to the pet that you are concerned specifically with that left foot of his/hers and trying to comfort that foot.

If you wanted to know why he/she is asking for your attention right now by making noise, you might create in your mind a cartoon of your pet barking or meowing, their mouth open, just as you would see the words "woof" or "meow" written in a balloon if you were reading a comic strip. Animals can readily respond to cartoon images sent telepathically.

As you make this Choice, even if your pet does not receive the picture you are trying to send in its mind, the pet will get the idea that you want to know something and may begin to get the impression that it has something to do with him/her – meaning that your communication is deepening.

For example, you might try making a drawing of the front door of your house and another picture of the door opening and the animal going outside if you would like them to go to that door and ask to be allowed to go out. Notice whether the animal does approach the door after you send them this message. Or you might create an image in your mind of cuddling your pet in a comforting affectionate manner. Notice if their behavior changes when you imagine these images. It can be a fun learning experience for both of you.

Or you might actually play a physical game of "hide and seek" with your pet. Place them out of the room and then hide their favorite toy in an unlikely place such as underneath a sofa. Then let them back into the room and say, "Where's your toy?" while at the very same time you mentally imagine him or her digging their paws under or sniffing under the sofa to find it where it is. Notice whether it's easier for your pet to find the toy quickly if you vividly visualize where it actually is. Practice should make it easier for the animal to catch your images sent telepathically through visualization and for you to create such images automatically when communicating to them.

If you are like most of us, you probably don't notice most of the fleeting images that come into your mind during the day unless they are especially vivid. This Choice will help you notice these images more closely and record their details. It is especially helpful if the image can be a little out of context and surprising. You may not be prepared for your pet's answers and expecting a surprise may allow you to be more flexible in receiving signals from them.

You will do better if you pursue this exercise with a sense of openness. Let your curiosity guide you. You are on an expedition into unknown territory and allow yourself to enjoy it.

Using Choices as you play with your pet, or in between practice sessions when you are alone with yourself, can teach you how to sense this more accurately when mental messages may be coming from the pet. You are learning to speak the pet's language as well as encouraging him/her to speak yours. This can deepen your relationship on all levels.

CHAPTER TWENTY

Getting Answers From A Pet

Here are two Choices that may help you elicit meaningful responses from your pet and can be soothing and healing for both of you:

You can say to yourself:

Choice #1

I choose to let what my animal wants to say to me easily pop into my mind."

Choice #2

"I choose to accept whatever (insert the name of your pet) has to say even if I don't really like what I'm hearing."

These Choices will lighten your own mood, which in turn will give your animal a reassuring emotional space in which to answer you and to cooperate with what it is you want him or her to do. It is in that space that the animal may begin to let you know what it is really feeling. Quietly saying to him/her something like, "Tell me more about this", is very useful. It will be encouraging on some level to the pet if you really are ready to hear what it has to say.

You may also find it useful to jot down in a notebook or on a pad of paper some of the random thoughts that come into your mind as possible answers to your questions. You can evaluate these later. The point is to simply get them down now while you're with your pet.

Some people report that they find it helpful to try breathing in unison with their pet even though respiration rates differ between humans and animals. If you want to try breathing momentarily at your pet's rate you can determine this by placing your hand lightly on their chest or upper abdomen. This can be a way of connecting with the animal and getting subtle signals from him/her that you might otherwise miss. In addition, it signals to the animal that you want to be in accord with him/her and that you will be able to hear what he/she have to say.

Some people who are quite untrained in communicating with animals have achieved some wonderfully helpful and often surprising answers when they ask the right kinds of questions of their pets. But if you don't get a direct answer that's all right too. You are still doing something that is useful for your pet by attempting to communicate. I can't emphasize often enough that if you do this periodically during the day, and for a number of days, something good will happen that is of a healing nature.

CHAPTER TWENTY ONE

Handling Guilt About A Pet

Here are some Choices that can help you if you feel guilty about anything you may have done (or failed to do) that you fear has harmed your pet:

Choice #1

"I choose to let go of my obsession with what is "right" or "wrong" in this instance, and know that there is no such thing as "right" or "wrong" in my pet's way of thinking."

This Choice honors the totally nonjudgmental nature of animals. There are certain things that concern every animal urgently such as food, shelter, warmth, and whether or not it is experiencing love– but animals have no concerns derived from judging and for this reason, there is no blame involved for anything you may have done or failed to do with respect to them. You can consider the situation as a slate wiped clean and replace your worry with good cheer and love for your pet and you'll be on exactly the same wavelength with them. Actually, you will be doing a great favor to your pet by doing this.

The following Choice may help with this:

Choice #2

"I choose to recognize that I am being given a wonderful chance to experience a positive, and deeply loving relationship with my animal right at this moment, (this is true, by the way, whether he/she is still alive or has passed on)."

This Choice recognizes the opportunity you now have to express great love for your pet by wiping away any need to dwell upon any difficulty between you. You will be eliminating any pain, guilt or remorse in yourself and cleaning the slate for their sake. Whatever either you or they did as part of creating the difficult circumstance you find yourself in, it can to be wiped clean – gone!

Choice #3

"I choose to learn from my pet's completely nonjudgmental attitude how I should act toward myself or others involved in this unfortunate incident."

Choice #4

"I choose to let my pet be my role model and learn from him/her the power of forgiveness."

CHAPTER TWENTY TWO

Dealing With A Lost Pet

As we indicated in the chapter on lost animals, locating an animal whose whereabouts is unknown is a complex, uncertain, extremely time-consuming and often frustrating process. Here are some Choices to use if you find yourself in this dilemma:

Choice #1

"I choose to speak quietly in my mind to my pet and tell (insert your pet's name) repeatedly that I am waiting for him/her to come home."

I suggest repeating this Choice to yourself frequently throughout the day, and to do so for as long as the animal is missing. Repetition should increase the chances of your pet receiving this message which could be very reassuring to him/her.

Choice #2

"I choose to picture opening my front door and seeing my pet there, perfectly normal and healthy, and watch as he/ she rushes into the house to his/her

familiar "places" to check out whether anything has changed since they were away."

Choice #3

"I choose to let my pet know that I am here for him/her just the way I was before."

Choice #4

"I choose to let my pet know that I want him/her to be safe and happy even before he/she gets home and that I am waiting for him/her with excitement."

CHAPTER TWENTY THREE

If Your Pet Has Passed Away

The following Choices are designed to help you lessen the pain of loss when an animal dies so that you can move through the normal stages of grieving more easily and perhaps soon be able to feel again the joy of having had this animal friend who inhabited your life so fully on earth for however long it remained here.

A Choice cannot take away your grief, nor should it try to, because grieving is an emotionally necessary stage we all must go through in order to recover from a deep personal loss - it is nature's way of restoring our life to some sense of balance- but the following Choices can help to prevent unnecessary side effects such as feeling guilty that you did not do enough to prevent your pet's death, feeling that you cannot face the future without your beloved animal, anger at fate for their death, or other unproductive reactions. You can also use Choices to help you learn the life lessons that your pets' passing holds for you, there are always some of these and they can be valuable.

Choice #1:

"I choose to view my animal's passing as having a positive meaning in my life that I do not yet understand."

Animal communicators have occasion to talk with thousands of departed souls of pets who have passed away. From doing this they gain a perspective that we cannot possibly have when we are confronted by a single loss and know only that our beloved animal is no longer present or that death may be imminent for it and this is extremely painful to know. Many seriously ill animals will tell an animal communicator whom their owner has consulted quite matter-of-factly, however, that it is their time to die and be truly comfortable with this fact.

In fact, it is many communicators' impression that animals will not allow their passing to be prevented if they are ready for it and their time "has come" to die. If the owner takes extraordinary measures in a hopeless situation their efforts will be futile because one way or another the animal will pass away if it is their time to do so, perhaps by an accident or through an attack by a predator. Not infrequently, its reason for withdrawing may be to help their beloved humans in some lesson that they need to learn in life, such as opening their heart more than it has ever been opened before, finding a deep value in their own life when they realize the true value of their pet to them, etc. There is always deep concern and closeness with those still on earth even though a pet has passed on as you have seen in the stories recounted in this book, and animal communicators report an impressive number of instances where animals have attempted to help from the other side.

In short, trying to do everything possible to help your animal medically to survive can be crucial in saving their life it that is what is intended for it, but if the animal is ready to die then it will only be futile and make the passing difficult for your pet rather than a rite of passage to be greeted with interest and a loving goodbye to you. In a sense, if the animal is comfortably ready to die and it is their "next step", you can help him or her best by going along with this as constructively as possible.

Here is a Choice you can make to help you see your animal's passing as quite out of your hands:

Choice #2

"I choose to let go of the illusion that this passing was (is) in my hands in any way and leave behind any resistance I may have about 'letting it happen'."

Another important Choice encourages your recognition of the fact that after your pet passes on, according to almost all animal communicators I know or have read about, the pet is now experiencing their own personal version of "heaven". This may not be what you have been taught to believe "heaven" is, but it is apparently in many ways a beautiful and happy existence for your animal. Probably the only thing that may be bringing down your pet from his or her buoyant sense of joy at this time is their concern for your well-being. The following Choice, repeated often, can be helpful in allowing you to feel more comfortable with their passing.

Choice #3

"I choose to know that my pet is happy in the afterlife and at the same time remains lovingly by my side in spirit."

The next Choice helps you to not interfere with the free will of animals and allow them to choose their own time and even their own way of passing over. It will help you realize that the large majority of reports from animal communicators tell us that animals do not report a fear of dying such as we humans experience and actually, for the most part, feel fine this with this event.

If an animal companion has just recently passed away, a close animal friend may choose to join it soon after this animal passes into the spirit world, but it is apt to do this from a wish to share a new adventure with the departed loved one, rather than from despair. It is rarely, as we might expect it to be from a human perspective, out of a feeling that the pet cannot bear to live on this earth without their dear friend, but often quite the opposite. Animals tend to see happiness as being in the present and do not want to remain emotionally attached to sad or frightening events that may have happened before their passing. In this respect, they have a great lesson to teach us who are human in terms of living in the present and looking forward to good things at all times instead of dwelling on bad ones.

To help yourself realize this in the case of a departed pet, here is another Choice to use.

Choice #4

"I choose to know that (insert your departed pet's name) is truly okay with what happened – whatever that was."

The next Choice has to do with being able to comfortably let your animal move along on a path which they experience at this moment as actually a happy and good one. Your love for your animal can greatly help you in doing this. Adding to all the good things you did for your pet during their lifetime you can now continue to help them by setting them free, knowing that freedom for them does not mean a severance of your eternal bond with them., but quite the opposite, that this bond is so strong it cannot be broken.

Choice #5

"I choose to allow (insert pet's name) to move along their path happily with tail wagging (purring, or

nuzzling, or doing whatever its species likes to do to express joy and contentment)"

And here is a Choice is to help you realize that so often our animals bring us life lessons that are precious beyond description and perhaps to help you have an inkling of what that lesson – their gift to you– might be for you in a given instance as they pass away.

Choice #6

"I choose to find a precious life lesson for me that lies within (insert your pet's name) passing."

Please use any or all of the Choices offered in this section liberally. It can make a true difference.

(If you want to learn more about how to construct effective Choices on your own, you will find information on how to do this in Part Three - the Resources Section of this book).

PART THREE

THE RESOURCES SECTION

CHAPTER TWENTY FOUR

Recommendations

This section of the book offers you some useful ways to expand the understanding of your pets that may have begun for you while reading these pages.

It is by no means an exhaustive exploration of the resources available in the areas listed here but represents my own (Dr. Patricia Carrington's) professional recommendations which I share with Karen Anderson.

Keep in mind that because I recommend a particular resource does not mean that there may not be other equally valuable resources that I don't know about. I do this simply to help you expand the information that is covered in this book.

1. To Schedule a Personal Consultation with an Animal Communicator

There are many fine Animal Communicators whom your friends or colleagues may be able to recommend for you, perhaps because they have used them. Here are two whom I can personally recommend highly, based on my personal/professional acquaintance with their work:

Karen Anderson: www.animalcommunicating.com

Danielle Mackinnon: www.daniellemackinnon.com

2. To Contact a Pet Who Has Departed

To reconnect with a pet now in the spirit world, through a personal consultation, I recommend both Karen Anderson's and Danielle Mackinnon's services as excellent:

Karen Anderson:
www.animalcommunicating.com

Danielle Mackinnon:
www.daniellemackinnon.com

3. For Reuniting with a Departed Loved One, Whether Animal or Human, *on Your Own*

For this purpose, I recommend Gil Alan's CONTACT, an outstanding short course available online. It guides you through a simple process which reunites you with a departed loved one rapidly and safely. Once you have undergone this CONTACT experience for the first time, you will have opened a door to communicate with spirit at any time with ease and you will be in control. Gil Alan is a spiritual leader to whom I give the highest recommendation.

For Information go to: www.GilAlan.com

4. For Expanding Your Use of the Choices Method

Although you have learned the Choices Method in a limited manner in this bookto use for your pets, but it can be immensely valuable to you personally as well. You can apply "Choices" to treat an extensive list of common emotional or physical problems such as anxiety, depression, physical illness or pain, relationship difficulties, addictions and many other distressing conditions. It is also highly effective for purposes of personal and/or spiritual development. To learn how to use it for your own self, I recommend my readable and authoritative book on this subject:

The EFT Choices Manual: Introducing the Positive into EFT by Patricia Carrington, Ph.D. (See "Products" at patcarrington.com)

You can also buy recorded products on the use of the Choices Method for selected personal growth and inspirational purposes at: patcarrington.com/all-products/specialized-eft-training/

To Schedule Individual Consultations with Dr. Patricia Carrington

See patcarrington.com, "The Power of Inner Guidance" on the Home Page of this website.

To Subscribe to my Free Newsletter On Energy Healing

My newsletter is entitled Energy Healing Updates. It provides stimulating articles and new techniques for you to use on the spot. You can subscribe by going to patcarrington.com.

To Purchase Karen Anderson's Book "Hear All Creatures"

This book was written before the publication of the book you are reading. It gives you 34 additional new stories of encounters with pets and can be purchased from Amazon.com in both Softcover and Kindle edition.

To Awaken Your Inner Guidance

This is the Online Training I mention in Chapter Three, which I used personally to develop my own Inner Guidance, and which radically changed my life as well as my professional career. This high level 8-Week Workshop is taught online by spiritual leader, Gil Alan, and pushes the doors of perception wide open – a true expansion experience for anyone looking to communicate with spirit and transform all areas of their lives on the highest level.

For information on the Awaken Your Inner Guidance Workshop www.GilAlan.com

To Learn About the Safe-Laser
for Animals and Humans

This safe-laser is the healing tool I used for my cat, Dandy when he was in pain from his cancer (see chapter two). To find out about and/or order one see goo.gl/ GGJwM6

To Learn to Communicate
with Animals on a Professional Level

Animal Communicators Karen Anderson and Danielle Mackinnon both offer high-level online courses in animal communication. Danielle's course can lead to a full certification program for those who want to become professional Animal Communicators.

Karen Anderson:
www.animalcommunicating.com

Danielle Mackinnon's
School of Animal Communication
animalgurus.com

Warmly,

Pat Cunnington